Repton

Reality

and Prayer.

Reality
and
Prayer

A GUIDE TO THE MEANING AND PRACTICE OF PRAYER

by John Magee

London
Hodder & Stoughton

Copyright © *1957, 1958 by John Magee*
FIRST PRINTED IN GREAT BRITAIN 1958

Printed in Great Britain for
Hodder and Stoughton Limited, London
by Lowe and Brydone (Printers) Limited,
London, N.W.10

To my Mother

LILLIAN NEWHOUSE MAGEE

Foreword

    In my opinion this is a great book. I hope it will win the recognition which it deserves. My own mind has been greatly enriched by reading the manuscript. There is so much in it that is worthy of repeated readings and the most serious study. Indeed, its greatest value is that of a stimulus, not only to understanding prayer, but to practicing it in the ways suggested.

    I have had the great privilege of meeting the author and of having many talks with him during my visits in 1951 and 1954 to the College of Puget Sound, Tacoma, Washington, at which he is a professor of philosophy. I felt very attracted to his personality, with its grand sense of humor and obvious sincerity. I feel proud that a Methodist minister has given twenty years of study, thought, and practice to equipping himself to write such a book. The background knowledge revealed in this book is, to me, staggering.

No reader should delude himself by supposing that this is merely another of the thousand books on prayer. This book is different. It leads into new depths of thought. It marshals evidence from new areas. Its insights again and again are startling in their orginality.

Prayer, of course, is a vast subject about which to write. One of our hymns says:

> Prayer is the simplest form of speech
> That infant lips can try.

Most of our praying takes advantage of that truth. But prayer is also the highest activity of man, and the reader who desires to leave prayer where that quotation leaves it will find little encouragement in this book. He may even be disconcerted by the complexities of prayer and of the long, arduous application it demands. We would, no doubt, rather read of the dramatic manifestations of God's presence and power. We like to think of symphonies and epics as being conceived and created spontaneously in an intense flame of intuition, and of saints becoming saints by virtue only of one overwhelming experience on some Damascus road. But any art from which great creations come has disciplines which would affright the novice if he could be made aware of them at the outset of his study; and we ought not to expect that the art of prayer can be mastered without due attention to the techniques which this book delineates. The author gives, of course, due regard and place to the workings of some unconscious superintellectual faculty, to the inspired moment out of time, and so on, but he does not see prayer as a principle of which one tablet, taken at bedtime and allowed to dissolve on the tongue, will ensure the inestimable, incomprehensible blessings of the Kingdom of God.

To be told to pray is boring and dull. But to be told how to pray, what techniques to follow, and what may be expected is surely one of the great needs of this distracted age. There is nothing conventional here, nor is there any folding of the hands in pious superiority, nor a recommendation to a kind of "mysticism *in vacuo*" which leaves so many of us bewildered.

John Magee lives in the modern world. He knows what is being said about it by the philosophers and psychologists. He knows what is being done in it by the scientists. (His chapter on "Science, Law, and Prayer" is the most valuable essay on that theme that I have ever read.) His chapter headings fulfill their promise, and through every chapter shines not only the wisdom of a disciplined and well-stored mind, but the insight and sympathetic realism of a man who walks with God.

LESLIE D. WEATHERHEAD

Minister of City Temple
London

Preface

This work began as a guide for personal use. In time, however, through my sharing it with students, parishioners, and fellow ministers, it grew into its present form. My debt to many is obvious.* One who works in this field is fortunately graced by many luminous names, the saints of many faiths.

I should like here to express my gratitude to my father under whose preaching I sat for twenty years; much of him is in these pages. Also, I should like to thank my wife, Kathryn, who read and reread the many drafts and never doubted that something good would come of it; the Reverend Dr. Leslie D. Weatherhead of City Temple, London, who urged me to write while the book was still in outline form and then generously contributed the Foreword; my colleagues at the College of Puget Sound, A.

* All sources and notes to material in the text have been placed chapter by chapter in the back of the book.

Kingsley Weatherhead and Leroy Ostransky, who also read the work in an early form and encouraged me in many ways. I should be remiss if I did not, furthermore, acknowledge the patient and substantial help offered me by the editors of Harper & Brothers.

My parishioners in the village of Gig Harbor, who during the past decade have patiently heard most of these ideas, deserve and have my heartfelt gratitude, as do students and fellow ministers who heard this material in lecture and urged its publication. Special thanks are due to Mrs. Dannis Dennis who typed the manuscripts and whose personal interest, encouragement, and careful work lightened the effort. Thanks for typing are also due to Miss Doris Andren.

JOHN MAGEE

College of Puget Sound
Tacoma, Washington

Contents

Reality

and Prayer

CHAPTER I

Prayer, the Church,

and Society

When Jesus swept clean the Temple at Jerusalem, he rededicated it as a "house of prayer for all nations." This the Church should be. It is the center of the highest and most vital spiritual forces and the temple in which man's longing for Reality may be satisfied. All the ecclesiastical machinery, theologies, creeds, and rituals are properly means to that end. The Church, the continuing incarnation of the body of Christ, has a function in creation which is not equaled by any other organization of life. That prime function is dependent upon the vitality with which the Church prays and worships.

From that praying, worshiping center flow those streams of life which are the Church's ministry to the world. Let us consider closely that ministry in its relationship to prayer.

Every society is based upon a conviction concerning the ultimate nature of things. The Church's primary ministry is to supply its culture with a continuous vision of the first principles by which alone men may live. When men forget, and they

periodically do, that their communal life is rooted in the super-
sensual, they become lost in greed, lust, or ambition, and the
social fabric is torn to pieces. T. S. Eliot says pointedly:

> What life have you if you have not life together?
> There is no life that is not in community,
> And no community not lived in praise of God.

Modern efforts to build a purely secular society are in futile
opposition to this principle of moral and spiritual togetherness
in the community. When secularism has at last divorced man
from his ultimate meanings, pulled him up by the roots and let
him wither above the life-nourishing ground, then the frantic
efforts to create an artificial community begin. These efforts
produce at last the compulsory social collectives of modern history. Seeking to restore the grace which was lost in man's aliena-
tion from God, they inevitably become religious in a demonic
way. The state then usurps the function of the Church and
brings curses rather than blessings.

But the Church itself is not immune to the general law of
decline in which persons and groups lose the first freshness of
the founder or great teacher. Let T. S. Eliot again state the issue:

> The Church must be forever building, for it is forever
>   decaying within and attacked from without;
> For this is the law of life; and you must remember that
>   while there is time of prosperity ·
> The people will neglect the temple, and in time of
>   adversity they will decry it.

The periodic cleansing and restoration of the Temple to its
proper uses are the responsibility of those who have recovered
for themselves the immediacy of spiritual experience and to
whom the teachings of religion become translucent windows
through which the light of heaven shines. The faith can really
never be defended: it must be reborn in fresh hope.

A tradition says that the night after St. Francis of Assisi had appeared before Innocent III to request his blessing on a proposed mission, the Pope had a dream. He saw the great Lateran Church, in which the Popes were crowned, falling apart. Deep cracks appeared in the walls. He cried out for someone to save the Church. Soon he heard the light, skipping sound of feet. Approaching the Lateran Church was Francis who seemed to grow at each step, until he encompassed the whole structure in his arms. The broken walls became quite strong again. This dream symbolizes the power of the spiritualized consciousness to restore the inner life of the Church and to redirect it to its divinely ordained tasks. But restoration is not enough. The past however vital always issues into the future.

The conservative, or conserving, function of the Church must be joined to its dynamic complement, prophetic religion. A society is a growing organism, not a static order. Prophetic religion has a feeling for the growing edge, where new rights are emerging and where new depths of fellowship and new forms of organization are required. To perform this purpose, prophetic religion often must employ a surgical criticism that probes infected areas and removes malignancies which would bring death. The courage and vision to accomplish these tasks come only to a person who has established himself in the deep certainty of faith. To be rooted in a constant awareness of God makes one unafraid of the world. Such rootage nourishes the ability to endure and to promote needed change, even the most radical change. In a day when there are so few unchanging and unchallenged aspects of our social life, such a prophetic quality is priceless. In the midst of the most hectic movements of peoples and forces it communicates the faith of Mother Juliana of Norwich that "all will be well, and all will be well, and all manner of thing will be well."

Some dimensions of the prophetic task are pointed out by

Charles Hendel of Yale University in his Rice lectures. He claims that only through a profound self-judgment on the idolatrous nationalism of our culture can we survive. Who is capable of such "epoch making doubtings"? Who is capable of a "successful assault and breaking the spell of the nationalistic religion of today?" He believes that only the religiously oriented man can do it. The celebrated sociologist Max Weber claimed that the religious power of the Reformation had to strike off the shackles of medievalism before the modern world could come forth. This prophetic action clears the way for other creative powers: "Philosophy, the arts, and the sciences can enter bringing their civilizing powers as they, too, have done before." But from what source doest this prophetic power flow?

The prophetic consciousness of the Church springs from adoration and confession. When the transcendent God is seen at the focus of life, all our fever of self-importance as a nation is merged into a larger perspective. We see the divine patience and the divine judgment. Confession is enlarged to include our whole community and perhaps even the whole civilization. "I am a man of unclean lips, and I dwell in the midst of a people of unclean lips." These words of Isaiah are the pained cry of one chosen for exacting prophetic work. But in these perplexed days the same holy Word commands us:

> Clear from the head the masses of impressive rubbish;
> Rally the lost and trembling forces of the will,
> Gather them up and let them loose upon the earth,
> Till they construct at least a human justice,
> The contribution of our star, within the shadow
> Of which uplifting, loving, and constraining power
> All other reasons may rejoice and operate.

Sometimes in deep prayer the prophet is overshadowed by a vision of what is to come, as though he were suddenly set squarely into the stream of time and knew its currents and directions. Such was the visionary consciousness of Isaiah's prefiguring of Christ; or Abraham Lincoln's envisaging of a new birth of freedom, or the inspiration of Walt Whitman, poet of democracy, when he wrote:

> I will make the most splendid race the sun ever shone upon,
> I will make divine magnetic lands
>   With the love of comrades,
>   With the life-long love of comrades.
> I will plant companionships as thick as trees along the
>   Rivers of America.

To the priestly and prophetic ministries of the Church we may add the ministry of reconciliation. Such a ministry seeks to create an atmosphere of agreement and harmony in the midst of human diversity, and the fostering of a climate of problem-solving rather than bitter competition or open violence. This requires the power to lay bare, in oneself as well as others, the intertwined bitter roots of conflict. Here grace must combine with worldly knowledge to analyze social and cultural situations, understand human motivations, and grasp the complexities of communication. Reconciliation requires, furthermore, the ability to appreciate truth in many diverse forms and to see and affirm the underlying unity of humanity in God.

The instrument of God in these prophetic matters may not be, probably will not be, a professionally religious person. He may be a mediator at points of international strife, or a social scientist pursuing his research into the complexities of racial conflict. But if he is working selflessly, seeking the unity of man at some deep spiritual level, he is a holy instrument.

Frank Laubach, celebrated teacher of world literacy, illustrates this reconciling ministry. When he went as a missionary to the Moros of the Philippines he was disappointed by a failure in

his professional life. While among people of another faith, he
began to renew his spiritual life through prayer. Gradually he
found a love of unexpected dimensions. Out of his study of the
native Moro religion emerged a realization that Islam's teaching
of "submission" to Allah (Moslem means "submitter") was an
authentic bowing down to the same Being whom he knew in
Christ. Gripped by this love and sense of spiritual unity, he found
it possible to serve their needs. As a result he invented his now-
celebrated system through which more people have been taught
to read and write than by any other method. For hundreds of
thousands he has created a written language and the beginnings
of a literature. Among the millions of colored peoples in Africa
and Asia, where there is so much bitter racial hatred, he is a white
man who is loved.

The same search for the spiritual unity of man applies to
intergroup harmony in management and labor and among nations and religions. It has been reported that Dr. Ralph Bunche's
method of arbitration in the Arab-Israel dispute of 1948 was to
supply indefatigably new alternatives and fresh possibilities for
agreement. Such creativity does not come from shallow, preju-
diced minds.

The true minister of reconciliation will thus possess insight
into authentic alternatives to violence. He will also have power
to soften the hardhearted. St. Francis, whose presence seemed to
invoke the Presence of the loving God, was able to end a hundred
years' quarrel on the steps of the Cathedral of Assisi. Gandhi,
who claimed that he never made even a minor decision without
prayer, aroused the compassion of both Hindu and Moslem, and
even commanded the love and respect of the English from whom
he wrested the most lucrative portion of their empire. John
Woolman, an eighteenth-century Quaker, traveled throughout
the American colonies and persuaded his fellow religionists to
liberate their chattel slaves. The record of his journeys is one of

the most remarkable of the whole antislavery movement. He aroused in slaveholders a longing to share his vision and passion for the welfare of the victims of the slave traffic. His influence stemmed from the loving prayer by which he carried those whom he visited to a new perception of love and a reawakening of conscience.

Intercessory prayer is an aspect of this reconciling ministry. We need to believe that God will work through His praying Church to heal and restore all life. Teams of intercessors in churches should be trained to pray for the needy, the sick, the mentally distressed, the morally corrupt, and the spiritually dead. Intercession should become the climate of pastoral counseling, social service, evangelism, education, and the other spiritual services of the Church to the community. We have not realized the extent and range of prayer.

We need to enlarge our intercession beyond the circle of those with whom we can sympathize because we see their pain. The priest in Graham Greene's *The Power and the Glory* epitomizes our limitation. Facing death in prison, he tries to pray. There are many for whom he wishes to pray, but the face of his own unhappy child blots out all other thoughts. Then with a powerful movement of love he prays: "O God, help her. Damn me, I deserve it, but let her live for ever." Such is the compassion with which we should pray for those we love. But he immediately reflects that "this was the love he should have felt for every soul in the world: all the fear and the wish to save concentrated unjustly on the one child." He tries again to pray for all those other endangered souls, "but in the moment of prayer he switched back to his child beside the rubbish dump, and he knew it was only for her that he prayed."

It takes long training to pray with power for such leaders of distant affairs as Presidents, Congressmen, United Nations Assemblies, and foreign statesmen. It takes even greater intensity to bring all the suffering folk of the world, friend and enemy alike, before God in intercession. God is waiting for a Church which will do this. Through such a circulation of the Spirit the whole climate of the world might be changed. Then the other healing forces of culture, trade, negotiation, learning, and the rest will be released from the downward spiral of ruin.

Beyond these three—the ministry of the priest, the prophet, and the reconciler—there is another prime function of religion that is intimately related to the work of prayer. This is the creation of the mature type of man who can live in the "brave new world" which has emerged in modern times. Let us consider some of his characteristics.

The man of prayer is able to stand alone. Whether in the concentration camp or in the life of a free community, the resources found in deep communion enable him to resist every tyranny from advertising to brainwashing and from all the subtle or direct pressures which make him conform or be silent. The only person who can resist to the end is one who knows that his life is rooted in an Eternity which is not merely a doctrine or belief but which is experienced inwardly. The monstrous tyrannies of our age all derive their power from ego-oriented fear, craving for comfort, or spiritual ignorance. In recent psychological studies of the relationship of personality to narrow and destructive ideologies, Frankel-Brunswik and others have concluded: "An individual is most receptive to those ideologies which afford the fullest expression to his over-all personality structure. Thus, a person clinically described as strongly authoritarian, projective, and destructive is likely to be receptive to an antidemocratic ideology such as . . . fascism . . . because it expresses his needs so well." But necessary as is this immunity to social pressure, it is not enough. To it must be joined a sense of solidarity with one's fellows.

The ability to stand alone is paralleled by the ability to stand with others and to give and receive love freely without guilt. True love requires that the lover be moved by genuine reverence and respect and not from a longing to make up for some childhood deficiency or ego-lack. According to the psychologist A. H. Maslow, individuals motived by such deficiencies cannot love; they must possess and exploit. They, furthermore, contribute to the disintegration of the social fabric. To balance the growing number of people deficient in this way society needs men who love on a vast scale, men who have sounded their own depths in confession and who in their actions reflect an outgoing reverence for life that springs from union with the Author of life.

The social need, then, is for a deeper charity, an invulnerable inner freedom from social coercions, and a confident faith in the spiritual premises upon which alone the common life may rest. To modern sensate man, hypnotized by sensory rewards and punishments, the man of prayer is the chief reminder of these invisible yet quite indispensable foundations. His life is the most powerful proof that they are Real. From him meaning overflows into every compartment of life and saves it from futility.

So, for example, prayer enables a man to see his own work as God's calling. The daily job and all other actions become a sacramental relationship to God. Our highly organized and mechanized workaday world has almost completely deprived us of a sense of individual contribution. What we do does not seem to count for much in the vast systems of factory, business, school, or church. This sense of futility yields in the life of prayer to a new orientation. We no longer do our work for man, but for God. He sees our labor and accepts it, and we offer to Him the fruits of all that is accomplished. Businessmen, labor leaders, diplomats, and folk in every walk of life need that same assurance in a form that is congenial to their own conceptions of the Spiritual. They have direct access to it in prayer.

On the morning of his death, the priest in Graham Greene's *The Power and the Glory* "felt only an immense disappointment because he had to go to God empty-handed, with nothing done at all. He knew now that at the end there was only one thing that counted—to be a saint." The only thing that ever counts is to be the instrument of the creative, loving, self-giving Will of God. Everything else becomes sheer futility.

Do you want the secret of a holy life? Do you want the strategy for a truly humane world? God has given us prayer, but whether or not we pray is entirely up to us. As Aldous Huxley says:

> *The choice is always ours.* Then, let me choose
> The longest art, the hard Promethean way
> Cherishingly to tend and feed and fan
> That inward fire, whose small precarious flame,
> Kindled or quenched, creates
> The noble or ignoble men we are,
> The worlds we live in and the very fates,
> Our bright or muddy star.

CHAPTER 2

Science, Law,

and Prayer

No modern treatment of prayer is complete without some clarification of its relationship to prevailing scientific notions, especially those we call "laws of nature." Living in these times automatically infects us with certain dominant philosophical and scientific ideas, many of which are hostile to the life of prayer. These assumptions about life and the universe lie deeper than consciousness and emerge in numerous ways to block our devotion. We ask such questions as: How can I expect God to answer prayer in a universe ruled by mechanical law? Does not our control of nature through science make prayer unnecessary? Why should we ask God for the things we can secure for ourselves through intelligent action? Science seems to have made prayer both absurd and unnecessary.

Our trouble with these questions is deepened by our double-minded attitude toward science and the scientific conception of the universe. On the one hand, science seems good, because natural law supplies us with reliable order. But on the other hand, science raises doubts not only about prayer, but about freedom, love, reason, and responsibility, indeed about the reality of the entire inner personal life.

In our era an immense liberation has been made possible by scientific advance. A thousand years of accumulated rubbish, which men had been told they must believe, has been disposed of. Sentimentality and unchecked fancy have been replaced by obedience to facts gleaned through patient inquiry. In spite of our Christian allegiances, we recall that the Christian vision of life, at least in its medieval version, blinded men to those common facts of existence which men trained in science were later to recognize. And how useful these facts have become! All the comforts of modern living rest upon this foundation of nature's transformation through scientific intelligence. In the middle of the last century, Thomas Henry Huxley, sensing the promise of the new science of medicine based upon bacteriology, was to ask with telling effect, "Is it morality that keeps the plague from our cities?" Our answer to that question is now vastly more complex, for with the development of atomic power we are not so sure that scientific medicine balances the immoral use of the weapons of war. Not only our cities, but the whole habitable world is threatened by these products of scientific inquiry.

But this is not the most troubling development. The growth of the sciences of man has extended the mechanistic interpretation of nature to ourselves. Man's history, personal and collective, loses the meaning which was rooted in his creativity and freedom. The idea of direction or purpose in events is replaced by a cosmic machine. "The world moves . . . on its metalled ways of time past and time future."

All this has had a shocking effect upon our religious consciousness. We have found gradually that our religious world picture, rooted in Biblical concepts of nature and man (all of them pre-scientific), has become antiquated and unbelievable.

However, in this mid-twentieth century several revolutionary developments in science place these queries in a new light. A new climate of thought is emerging. To attempt to replace new concepts of the universe for those which have been unquestioned in our culture for more than two hundred years may seem like folly. However, such an undertaking is necessary in order to remove so formidable a barrier to the practice of prayer. Furthermore, rapidly accumulating evidence in the sciences is making such a change in thought inevitable. We will sketch three major developments in twentieth-century science which I firmly believe will prove to be fertile soil for the growth of modern devotion.

The first of these major developments in scientific and philosophical thought promises to modify fundamentally the picture of iron mechanistic law and to replace it with a view of reality that is organismic. According to this view the universe is composed of living substances organized within other living substances.

Developments in atomic physics have forced scientists to abandon the hope of applying mechanistic "cause and effect" explanations to the ultimate particles of matter. Atomic events seem to obey a law of "wholeness." This means that every part of the atomic event is in organic connection with the rest. We are left with the strange, though experimentally established fact, that we cannot "predict" exactly what will happen until the event is past. The last moment of the event seems to have important effects upon the initial moment. Where a particle is going is as important as where it has been. All the forces in the situation seem to be operating throughout the whole system just as in a living body. In *Science and the Modern World*, Whitehead refers to this as "the brooding presence of the whole onto its various parts."

Proposing this same organic interrelatedness of physical events, Max Planck, celebrated physicist and discoverer of the quantum theory, writes: "It is impossible to obtain an adequate version of the laws for which we are looking, unless the physical system is regarded *as a Whole*. According to modern mechanics, each individual particle of the system, in a certain sense, exists simultaneously in every part of the space occupied by the system. This simultaneous existence applies not merely to the field of force with which it is surrounded, but also to its mass and its charge."

In the eighteenth century, before the rise of these organic concepts of physical nature, the astronomer Laplace could assert: "If for a single instant an intelligence were to be acquainted with all the forces by which nature is animated and with the positions of all the particles that compose it, and if this intelligence should be capable of submitting all these data to rational analysis, it would represent by one and the same formula the movements of the largest bodies in the universe and those of the smallest atom." He draws the inevitable conclusion from such a world view: To such an intelligence "nothing would be uncertain . . . the future as well as the past would be open to its inspection."

We now know that hope for this type of mechanical prediction is baseless and that Laplace's supermind would not be able to predict on the basis of the information he indicates, for the intimate commerce of events on the smallest scale simply does not follow mechanical patterns.

On the contrary, the natural sciences have reached a critical turning point which alters all our former scientific conceptions and makes us skeptical of interpreting reality in terms of them. Summarizing this present position of science, Whitehead claims, "The stable foundations of physics have broken up: also for the first time physiology is asserting itself as an effective body of knowledge, as distinct from a scrap-heap. The old foundations of scientific thought are becoming unintelligible. Time, space, matter, material, ether, electricity, mechanism, organism, configuration, structure, pattern, function, all require reinterpretation." And then to lay the ghost of any lingering eighteenth-century astronomers who cling to Laplace's theory of mechanical prediction, he writes, "What is the sense of talking about a mechanical explanation when you do not know what you mean by mechanics?" Such is the upshot of present inquiries in the physical sciences. And when we venture into other departments of science we find more to support our interpretation.

An exploration of the so-called "border line" between living and nonliving substance makes the organismic view of the universe even more plausible. Upon close inspection those interesting crystals called "viruses" betray in an elementary form the characteristics of living bacteria. The more closely we inspect the actual organization of the so-called nonliving substances in their minutest constituents, the more they appear to obey living rather than mechanistic laws. That is, they operate as wholes, partly self-determining, giving at times the appearance of a "society" of minute organisms rather than a mechanical collection.

In the light of such findings we may be well justified in assuming that even in so-called nonliving matter there is feeling and awareness, however dim or minute, and that behind the outward appearance of mechanism is a "subjectivity" which corresponds in some remote way to our consciousness. Each genuinely organic unit, an atom, say, or a molecule or crystal, will have something analogous to our feelings, powers of self-direction, selective response to the environment, and the like, though, of course, in a very minimal way. The entire physical world is simply a collection of such living entities. There is no matter which is merely dead machinery. At points, for example, in plants, animals, and our bodies these organisms are collected into larger living wholes. In such cases the smaller organism is controlled in part by laws of its own and in part by the laws of the more inclusive organism. Whitehead points out, "Molecules differ in their intrinsic character according to the general organic plan of the situations in which they find themselves."

If the physical world is thus made up of living parts, a question arises. How shall we account for the mechanistic features of our experience and for the laws of large-scale mechanics as they appear in astronomy or geology? Why does the world, on certain levels of scientific observation, appear to be a machine? The most plausible answer seems to be that such laws are "statistical," that is, they are the average performance of billions of living entities, each of which obeys its own living law.

An illustration from Karl Heim's *The Transformation of the Scientific World View* will help clarify this idea. Suppose a company of soldiers is marching on the drill ground. Each soldier is a free, living person whose behavior is temporarily subject to the ordering command of an officer. From an airplane high enough to obscure the individual soldiers, the troop movements would appear indistinguishable from a machine.

Consider another illustration, the actuarial table of an insurance company. By taking the average age of every person who dies, say, in the United States, it is possible to discover the "life expectancy" of the American population. Insurance premiums can be calculated on the basis of a figure set at seventy years. If the company loses money on a few who die young, it will make money on those who live beyond the expected age. In the end, the effect is the same as though they had all lived just seventy years. This makes insuring a scientific business. However, it gives us no information whatsoever about the life expectancy of any one person. The laws which determine how long any one of us shall live are biological, not actuarial. No one's death is ever "caused" by the actuarial table. It is not a law of individuals, but a statistical average.

The mechanical laws of physics and chemistry are statistical in the same sense. They are the averages of the actions of the organic units which constitute the world of living nature. These laws are more certain than any social statistics because of two facts: The organisms making up the material bodies are so rudimentary that they have less freedom than human beings. And, beyond this, there are so many of them. There are billions of billions of them in a cubic centimeter. In these swarming myriads, the deviation of a few individuals scarcely affects the general outcome.

What bearing does this all have on prayer? These modern developments at once set aside the old mechanistic picture of reality which made prayer a logical absurdity. The old eighteenth-century concept of nature as "a dull affair, soundless, scentless, colourless; merely the hurrying of material, endlessly, meaninglessly," is repudiated, and a living nature akin to mind and spirit is put in its place. The men of the eighteenth century, whose hatred of Gothic architecture, Whitehead says, "symbolizes their lack of sympathy with dim perspectives," were the fashioners of the mechanistic world picture. Their view seemed clear and almost overwhelming to common sense. But their reason was "one-eyed reason, deficient in its vision of depth." What is given to us by their modern successors is a nature that is vaguer but richer, more mysterious, more alive and purposive. Such a nature is vastly more congenial to the spiritual life and makes prayer an exciting possibility.

Our own bodies are a parable of nature. They are made up of living cells, each with a life cycle of its own. Yet these cells are caught within the over-all ordering power of the body and thus behave in such a way as to build up the functioning of the body as a whole. Psychosomatic medicine describes the process by which some conflict or stress within the mental life produces disorder and pain within the body. Anxiety, for example, may cause ulcers or high blood pressure. This seems to occur through some disruption of the governance which the healthy mind en-

C

joys over the cells of the body. This governance has many analogies to a well-ordered civil state.

The universe can best be thought of in the same organismic terms. As far down as we care to go in the scale of being we discover a force analogous to this "life-field" at work. Rising in the scale we find plants and animals. Rising still further, we see that the universe exemplifies in personality, in societies, in solar systems and galaxies the same laws of wholeness. If we are correct in dismissing mechanistic laws as purely statistical, then the law of the universe—if it has any law at all—must be a living Will. The practice of prayer starts with this primary hypothesis: God is the being in whom all else exists. The ultimate character of all law is His will, and His life is the life of all.

In the light of these considerations the power of will over events becomes a perfectly natural occurrence, and prayer becomes a "normal" event. Let us consider the matter more closely. In the complex relationship between the will and physical events, four levels can be distinguished by means of our present knowledge. There is first the common-sense experience of commanding the body to perform tasks such as sitting or rising. Then, there is the power which a word of command has over the body of someone else when he is willing to obey. His actions are the indirect result of the will of the person issuing the command. There is, thirdly, the real though obscure influence of the subconscious upon the body. The fact of this relationship is the foundation of psychosomatic medicine which studies illnesses resulting from deep subconscious wishes or fears unknown to the patient. It is known, for example, that certain kinds of ulcers, hypertension, chronic rhinitis, and a growing catalogue of other illnesses may originate in subconscious mental states rather than in organic conditions.

The effect of the subconscious also appears dramatically in hypnosis when parts of the body are rendered insensitive to pain, or blisters are made to appear without actually burning the flesh. These same effects could not be produced by the hypnotized subject outside the hypnotic state. He needs the special circumstances of hypnosis to bring about the numbness or the lesions. Apparently there is some special focusing of the will in these states which accounts for the dramatic effects.

The fourth level on which the will affects events is in some ways the most mysterious of all, the power of the will to command matter outside any living body. Both J. B. Rhine of Duke University, North Carolina, and Robert Thouless of Cambridge University, England, have demonstrated that mechanically shaken dice can be unmistakably influenced by a person who wills that certain faces of the dice shall turn up. The amount of this influence has been statistically measured.

It is clear from these facts that the limits of willing which we experience on the conscious level need not be the real limits. In certain expanded or concentrated moments the will of man may exceed in result anything which we could have inferred from ordinary sense experience. The data of prayer experience reveals that in periods of high faith even the extraordinary results of hypnosis, psychotherapy, or psychokinesis are surpassed.

Returning to commonplace experience again, we discover that living events all require some kind of "faith" or "belief." The faith channel seems to be the route by which such occurrences are initiated. "If, as a healthy man," writes Karl Heim, "I give the order to carry out a particular movement to my hand or foot, I know that the order will be obeyed. It is entirely obscure to me how I reach this assurance. It does not rest on the fact that I know about the physiological nexus which obtains as between the cerebral cortex and the movements of my limbs, and that I am convinced from experience that the channels of transmission are in working order and that therefore the instructions can be carried out. Unless I have studied anatomy, I have no notion whatever about these inter-connections. Nevertheless, knowledge that the order will be carried out is undeniably there." We would like to know more about this mysterious assurance which permits us to do the most ordinary things. Karl Heim suggests, "This certainty is like something granted to me from hidden depths. Only if the knowledge is present am I able to will, and to give orders to my members. If I entertain doubts as to whether my hand or my foot will in fact obey me, which is what happens in certain states of paralysis, I am able only to wish that the movement might happen, but am not able to will it."

Modern physical and psychiatric medical practice acknowledges this peculiar function of the will by seeking to stimulate faith in the patient, arousing his deep will to recovery. The late Dr. Richard Cabot of Harvard likened the modern hospital, with its mysterious paraphernalia, esoteric vocabulary, and ordered routine, to the crosses and sacraments of healing shrines. The modern patient with his faith in "science" responds to the symbols as well as to the medicine. He is enabled to will beyond the previous limits of his consciousness and affect portions of his being formerly remote from his will power.

Turning from common sense and medical practice to experiences in prayer, we observe that when the channels of total willing are in order through deep faith and an intuitive contact with the depths of life, very great and "miraculous" events may occur. Jesus expressed this vividly: "Truly I say unto you: Whosoever shall say to this mountain, 'Bestir yourself, and throw yourself into the sea,' *and shall not doubt in his heart,* but shall believe that what he says comes to pass, he shall have it." Karl Heim clarifies this strange saying: "Jesus does not say that a particular man can transfer a mountain into the sea by uttering a magic word. He merely says that if every trace of doubt has been banished from the heart in respect of some event, then that event will take place. Clearly no one could utter such a ridiculous command without feeling doubt about its fulfillment. But it is precisely upon this 'not doubting' that everything depends. In other circumstances, where doubt could be completely banished success would not be lacking." Then returning to the universal characteristics of all willing both within and outside of prayer, he says, "Indeed, the certainty we enjoy in respect of everyday behavior is only possible because we are reaching out into the dark future with a clairvoyant assurance that what we resolve upon will indeed happen. This is the inner structure of every act of will."

The "clairvoyant assurance" to which Heim refers is an intuitive certainty arising out of the close communion of living entities. Such assurance comes in the body through the feeling of health and well-being among the cells of the organism. The faith, reaching beyond the body, that the connections of willing are in order and that the living world will respond, comes in like manner from the luminous darkness of deep feeling; from quietness and confidence; from much time spent in meditation upon kinship with the whole of life; from love and reverence for all living creatures; from the "prayer and fasting" which Jesus advised in hard cases; from casting oneself deeply into God and trusting the holy impulses which spring from His will.

When after such communion the movement of faith comes from the depths, then the word of faith becomes indeed a word of power. Our Lord said, "Believe that you receive it, and you will!" Such faith is not persuading oneself to believe something that he knows is not so!

To this point we have been concerned with the new picture of the universe suggested by the modern revolution in science. Let us turn to another aspect of the relationship between scientific law and prayer, the methods by which scientists formulate these laws rather than the laws themselves. The contemporary clarification of the true meaning of scientific method and the knowledge it yields, and does not yield, is as important a revolution in thought as the new world picture previously described.

All theoretical thinking is abstract. The thinker inevitably analyzes out of the concrete whole of experience those aspects which interest him and develops his theories accordingly. Each science is concerned with a different segment of the real world, not with the Real as a Whole.

Years ago, Sir Arthur Stanley Eddington, the distinguished British astronomer and writer on scientific themes, suggested this classic illustration. "Let us then examine the kind of knowledge which is handled by exact science. If we search the examination papers in physics and natural philosophy for the more intelligible questions we may come across one beginning something like this: 'An elephant slides down a grassy hillside. . . .' The experienced candidate knows that he need not pay much attention to this; it is only to give an impression of realism. He reads on: 'The mass of the elephant is two tons.' Now we are getting down to business; the elephant fades out of the problem and a mass of two tons takes its place. . . . Never mind what two tons refers to; what is it (for the physicist)? . . . Two tons is the reading of the pointer when the elephant was placed on a weighing machine. Let us pass on. 'The slope of the hill is 60 degrees.' Now the hillside fades out of the problem and an angle of 60 degrees takes its place. What is 60 degrees? . . . 60 degrees is the reading of a plumb-line against the divisions of a protractor. Similarly for the other data of the problem. The softly yielding turf on which the elephant slid is replaced by a coefficient of friction, which though perhaps not directly a pointer reading is of kindred nature.

"And so we see," concludes Eddington, "that the poetry fades out of the problem, and by the time the serious application of exact science begins we are left with only pointer readings."

The physicist is interested in the measurable aspects of reality which he calls "mass," "velocity," and "extension." Everything else he purposely leaves out. The biologist would certainly be interested in the elephant as a living entity, and the psychologist would seek the motives which led men to import elephants and little boys to pay money to see them. Each of these scientists would have a different body of data and laws.

Let us take another illustration. I say to my son, "John, please take your bicycle and get a loaf of bread from the bakery." Assuming that he does it, let us consider some of the many ways this event might be analyzed.

The *physicist*, as we have seen, would be interested in mechanical aspects: mass, speed, energy expended, and work done. A *biologist* would study the living organisms. The *psychologist* would look at the attitudes and inner needs of the persons involved: hunger, status, affection, and so on. The *social-psychologist* and *sociologist* would describe the event in terms of socially defined roles (father, son, merchant), the family and store as social institutions, and why the actors responded to these social demands in their particular ways.

If we go beyond the exact sciences, we discover other ways in which the occasion may be analyzed. In *ethics*, new questions, such as the rightness of the request or the fairness of the price of bread, would have to be answered. This might lead into socio-ethical questions concerning the justice of the economic system or the role of government in regulating pure food standards. If we were concerned with *aesthetics*, we would ask still a different set of questions. In terms of *religion* we would be interested in the reality of the relationship between father and son and the way in which each perceived his responsibility to the divine Order. Such things would be reflected in the way the request was made and the grace with which it was answered.

The problem we are wrestling with here, how prayer can be answered in a world of law, arose from the uncritical dogma that physics and its methods has complete priority over all other methods of rational inquiry, and that it alone can explain an event. This picture of the many levels upon which explanation may proceed liberates us from such a dogma. Even within a single science there are hierarchies of laws so that one law seems to overrule another. If we drop a piece of wood from a window and it falls to the ground, we speak of gravity. But if we carve the wood into a wing and tail fins, mount these on a light spindle and then toss our handiwork into the wind, it floats on the same air which before failed to support it. The wood flies. The law of gravity has not been violated; the principles of aerodynamics have been invoked.

When a doctor administers penicillin to a child suffering from a fever, the temperature goes down. Events in the body have been changed, but no law has been violated. If, after the child's illness has not responded to medical treatment, we pray, and if, in turn, her fever then leaves, no law has been violated. A new law has been exemplified.

Let us summarize the conclusions to this point: First, the number of ways in which the intellect may analyze a segment of the Real world is potentially infinite. Furthermore, no one of these special modes of intellectual analysis, scientific or nonscientific, has any special priority over the others. The particular mode of inquiry we employ depends upon the purposes to which we wish to put our conclusions. In the illustration given above, for example, a bicycle cannot be mended with moral categories, nor can a moral deficiency be amended by following the rules of mechanics. Lastly, we must insist that no one of these separate ways, nor all of them together, add up to the whole of Reality, for they are all abstract. We commit a major fallacy when we analyze from the whole an abstraction useful for some special purposes and then proclaim it alone to be the whole. Referring to the mechanistic world picture, Whitehead writes, "This conception of the universe is surely framed in terms of high abstractions, and the paradox only arises because we have mistaken our abstractions for concrete realities." The sciences are "simplified editions of matters of fact."

Eddington has insisted that the mathematical constructs of physics have about as much relationship to the nature of things "as a telephone number has to a subscriber." In the sciences of man this is even more evident. The records in the clinical file of an individual—his height, weight, and psychosomatic structure, his position in sociometric test, his scores on intelligence and personality tests of all sorts, his personal history file—do not constitute real knowledge of the man himself. If you would know him, you must meet him as a person, engage in manifold human relationships with him, make him a friend, and suffer with him. If you wish to illuminate these experiences through reflection, you will have to draw from a multitude of nonscientific disciplines. The web of scientific explanations simply does not capture the whole man.

Human personality is at the intersection of innumerable levels of reality, physical, biological, psychological, sociological, axiological, psychic, and spiritual. It is natural, then, that what happens to so complex a being as ourselves will not be understood except in terms of an enormously complex series of interactions in which "lower" levels are often overruled by "higher" ones. This was illustrated above when we "overruled" the law of gravity by making an airplane responsive to the laws of aerodynamics. In prayer such "overruling" occurs when we respond to the spiritual order which Jesus called the Kingdom of God. When men inquire as seriously into that Order as they have into the physical, we may expect a vast transformation in human life. "Miracle" will then be understood in Allan Hunter's words as "Christ's freedom to obey a higher law."

We have described the major revolution of scientific thought in our century which has led first of all to the emergence of an organismic view of physical reality, and secondly to a clearer understanding of the nature of scientific knowledge itself. A third area in which the climate of scientific thought is changing rapidly to make our mid-century a more hospitable environment for prayer concerns the motivations necessary for the continued existence of scientific inquiry as such. "Is it not possible," queries Whitehead, "that the standardized concepts of science are only valid within narrow limitations, *perhaps too narrow for science itself?*" The old scientific world picture would seem to make the continuing enterprise of science itself an impossibility. This can be seen at several crucial points.

First, scientific activity, like any other human enterprise, is moved by faith. The early scientists were animated by the assumption of a rational world order, a vision of reality derived from the prescientific reflections of philosophers and theologians of earlier periods. "The faith in the possibility of science, generated antecedently to the development of modern scientific theory," states Whitehead, "is an unconscious derivative from medieval theology." It is a faith in the rational governance of the world. Even where the more anthropomorphic elements of that governance are rejected, great modern scientists still have held to the essential assumption. "The longing to see this pre-established harmony," writes Einstein in defense of another great scientist of this century, "is the source of the inexhaustible patience and persistence which we see in Planck's devotion to the most general problems of our science, undeflected by easier or more thankful tasks. I have often heard that colleagues sought to trace this characteristic to an extraordinary will-power; but I believe this to be wholly wrong. The emotional condition which renders possible such achievements is like that of the religious devotee or the lover. The daily striving is dictated by no principle or programme, but arises from an immediate personal need." And Max Planck, writing of Kepler, Galileo, Newton, and other great scientists of the classical period, says, "For all these men devotion to science was, consciously or unconsciously, a matter of faith—a matter of a serene faith in a rational world order."

Turning from the visionary faith of the best scientists to a glimpse of their intimate experiences at the time of discovery and invention we discover how strangely "unmechanical" the progress of science has been. The creative moments of those who were responsible for the greatest scientific advances were not unlike those of artists, poets, novelists, and playwrights. The mind in creation is substantially the same whatever the subject matter. It is a question of brooding on a chaos of material until some unforeseen order and coherence emerge. The requirements for such creativity are faith, courage, and vision. They cannot be dispensed with no matter how "unscientific" they may appear. The attempt to do without them automatically relegates the thinker to the performance of third-rate chore work.

Thirdly, a mechanical world devoid of value, meaning, and purpose, if taken literally, would make scientific work impossible. "Many a scientist has patiently designed experiments," laments Whitehead, "for the purpose of substantiating his belief that animal operations (including human) are motivated by no purposes." He adds an ironic touch: "Scientists animated by the purpose of proving that they are purposeless constitute an interesting subject for study." Scientific activity is highly purposive, and simply because one of its chief purposes is to exclude purpose from its sphere of study should not blind us to that fact. Any view of reality which does not make sense of the scientist and his activity must be false and could only by an ironic twist be called "scientific."

Even Bertrand Russell, who denies any moral purposes in nature, decries the gradual disappearance of aesthetic values from the scientific view. Writing of the loveliness of sound and color, he mourns, "All these things have been transferred from the beloved [nature], to the lover [man], and the beloved has become a sketleton of rattling bones, cold and dreadful, but perhaps a mere phantasm." But these very aesthetic values have functioned importantly in scientific thinking. The mathematician Jacques Hadamard, having made studies of this element in the history of science, concludes that in many crucial cases aesthetic feeling more than any other factor determined the selection of both the subject matter and the type of theoretical explanations which were acceptable. On the applied level, to be sure, practical considerations often look large, but at the level where scientific advances have been made it is astonishing how little men were concerned with the usefulness of their work. They were moved by its beauty, its intrinsic value, and its power to satisfy a cosmic curiosity. When science becomes too literal-minded in believing its "simplified edition of matters of fact," and its devotees lose their poetic vision and their sense of deep communion with nature in all its aspects, there is danger that scientific advance itself will grind to a halt.

Finally, science is conducted by groups of men and requires great moral power for its organization. Mechanistic materialism would rob man of this quality. The tragic paradox of this type of development is indicated in another of Bertrand Russell's observations: "Science, which began as the pursuit of truth, is becoming incompatible with veracity, since complete veracity tends more and more to complete scientific skepticism." Skepticism is not fertile ground for those qualities of self-sacrifice, good will, and courage which are indispensable for the scientific enterprise. Without these qualities the scientist becomes a black-magician seeking understanding only to enhance his power. "As soon as the failure of science considered as metaphysics is realized," writes Russell, "the power conferred by science as a technique is only obtainable by something analogous to the worship of Satan, that is to say, by the renunciation of love." When this amorality of the skeptical view of life overtakes not only the scientists, but the philosophers, artists, politicians, industrialists, and labor leaders, then we shall have reached the point where the insufficiency of narrow scientific concepts has become tragically evident.

This survey makes clear the need of science for the spiritual renewal which can come through profound prayer: an experience of spiritual immediacy which restores depth to reason; recaptures glimpses of beauty, truth, and goodness to refresh the roots of inquiry; revives the image of wholeness, from which the scientific picture was first torn by its method of abstraction; and restores the whole man to his place in a holy universe.

In our work thus far we have seen that prayer is the essential undergirding for the main functions of religion and that science, far from barring the way to prayer, calls for a fresh exploration of the spiritual basis of man's life in this mysterious universe. But before we can turn to the meaning and practice of prayer itself we must look at yet one further problem, unanswered prayer.

CHAPTER 3

The Problem

of Unanswered Prayer

Sometimes our prayers are not answered. This fact has
put a stop to the praying of many men and has caused an
agonizing perplexity for others. Parents pray for a sick child and
he dies; a wife sees her husband sicken and die in the prime of
life in spite of her prayers; a church prays for a youth in deep
need, and no answer seems to come. What shall we say to these
persons?

Our reply depends upon the nature and mood of the one who
has had such experiences. The brokenhearted person becomes
angry with God or bitter toward the Church for teaching what
now seems to have proven false. He needs loving counsel until
the angry and bitter feelings subside and the matter can be
freshly appraised. The skeptic who has been waiting for his
"evidence" probably says to himself, Just as I thought. He needs to
be reminded that the skeptical way of life makes decisive proof of
spiritual realities impossible. Only when a man begins to doubt
his doubts and ventures beyond them toward a more exacting

encounter with existence will faith in the reality of Spirit emerge. Only then is he prepared to test prayer and evaluate its results. A man risking his life in humble and loving trust in the unseen Real will discover his doubts progressively resolved and the claims of prayer abundantly verified. Our discussion of unanswered prayer is for these reasons not for the skeptic nor for the person disturbed by overwhelming disappointments. It is pointed rather to the person venturing in the life of faith, who has no doubt known answers to prayer, and who is now baffled by an unexpected and inexplicable rebuff.

We often fail to receive answers to our prayers, because, as St. James writes, "You ask wrongly." We still have much to learn about the spiritual Order and our interaction with it. John Gaynor Banks writes, "God is no respecter of persons, but he is a respecter of conditions. We must learn to supply these conditions more effectively." God is not arbitrary. The world He has created is a living world with definite types of structures and relationships, and prayer that is out of harmony with this reality will be unanswered, no matter how much we wish it.

It was this belief that prayer had to meet certain conditions that nearly twenty years ago set me to the task of discovering the laws of prayer. Unanswered prayer should be a challenge to our Christian intelligence just as uncured disease is a challenge to medical research. In the most reverent sense of the word, this is an invitation to more knowledge and skill.

When the disciples after their experience on the Mount of Transfiguration failed to heal the epileptic boy, they went to Jesus privately to inquire why they had failed. He did not put them off by saying that they were asking blasphemous questions. "This kind," he told them, "cannot be driven out by anything but prayer." Apparently he had learned in his own experience that such cases would yield only to him who had spent sufficient time in prayer.

We should not give up our faith in the promises of prayer because of failures. We should first suspect some failure in ourselves. In other areas of human knowledge we do not discard so easily what we have been taught. The bride who follows the tested recipe and almost gags her husband does not lose faith in recipe books or cooking. She discerns a failure in her own lack of skill. Students who were demonstrating the law of diffusion of liquids by putting copper sulfate crystals into two jars of water, one hot and the other cold, did not lose faith in the law of diffusion or the truths of chemistry because the results were contrary to what the chemistry book predicted. They assumed a failure of technique. A second failure shook them no more than the first. We should remember that a long tradition of spiritual lore, in which many conditions have been laid down, has been validated in experience. Our failures should humble but not defeat us.

The search for the proper "ways" of prayer, for adequate technique, interpreted in the broadest sense must continue. The life of faith demands it. Nevertheless, we should note that it is not possible, merely by the mastery of technique, to create in music, poetry, or science. And the same is true in prayer. There are no easy tricks in the realm of the creative spirit. The art of prayer, like the art of any other creative work, is partly mysterious. The poet, even the greatest poet, does not always write a good poem, nor the greatest preacher deliver a fine sermon. This is what distinguishes art from science. These arts lie in the realm of spirit where the relationships include freedom and response and where we are not manipulating objects but dealing with values and persons, or perhaps, as in prayer, with ultimate values and the Supreme Person. There is no denying that there are conditions to be learned and failures in technique to be corrected, but the improvement of method, however profound, cannot turn into magic which guarantees results in advance.

Sometimes the failure of prayer can be traced neither to a failure of technique nor to a deficiency of spirit, but the power of prayer is blocked by the attitudes of others. In Nazareth, Jesus "could do no mighty works" because of their unbelief. God's intention was the same toward the Nazarenes as toward the Samaritan leper who was healed, and Jesus was the same Son doing the Father's work, but the results were twisted and blocked by his fellow townsmen who were blind to the presence of the holy power.

Even in situations such as these, however, God's sovereign love is expressed with power. St. Paul writes, "Nothing you ever do for Him is lost." In the Garden of Gethsemane Jesus asked three times to have the cup pass, and he prayed with his whole heart. But he knew before he left the Garden that the request was denied, so he withdrew it. In response, God did something greater than saving his life. He let the power of those mighty petitions be displayed in the manner of his death and rising. It may be hard for us to believe, especially at the time of disappointment, but, if God is indeed the father of our Lord Jesus Christ, this will happen with every petition denied us, provided we accept as totally as Jesus did the "No" that came at Gethsemane.

Such a "No" may be a necessary reminder that God is not accountable to us. He is *Mysterium Tremendum*" as well as Father. He is the enigmatic mystery which limits us on all sides. He is the vast inscrutable, as well as the near and dear. His way will not always be our way, and we will not know why. In fact, we would probably not be capable of understanding His why. Honesty in the life of prayer does not require that we know the answer to these things any more than we are required to know all the mysteries of personhood before we fall in love or beget children.

Another fact that we should recognize in understanding unanswered prayers is that prayer is at some point limited in the

D

order of God. It would be useless, in my opinion, to pray to restore an amputated leg. I believe that prayer focuses primarily on those aspects of existence which are dynamic and growing, the turning points or growing edges of life. The great semirigid processes, such as the solar system, are not areas for prayer action. They are rather the firm stage upon which our lives are acted out. Prayer is limited in another way in the order of God. It is not our only form of co-operation with Him. Sacrificial work, persuasion, loving co-operative action, building institutions, adding to knowledge, and accumulating and distributing wealth are likewise necessary.

The area of health is a good example. Medical science can advance only through research, unselfish service, the building and management of hospitals and schools, and the development of economic arrangements for distributing health services. Health also requires good food and the organization of agriculture. It requires a reasonable income, widely enough distributed to make possible the purchase not only of health services but also food, clothing, leisure, and education. Much illness is due to poverty, war, or other forms of social decay. We cannot expect prayer to wipe out miraculously the accumulated results of these long unsolved problems. It would be foolish to imagine that prayer makes all this complicated co-operation unnecessary. We will pray for the sick with our whole hearts, but many times God will ask us to wait upon these other forms of co-operation with Him. Often the demand for and the direction of that co-operation will come out of prayer itself.

Sometimes the problem of unanswered prayer is phrased differently. Can I be living completely in God's Kingdom of wholeness if I still retain some physical or psychological disability? Is my defect a sign that I am not living in Christ and he in me? Is it a proof of some secret sin or unforgiven area of resistance to God's will?

Let us grant that God's purpose is wholeness and perfection. Yet I am convinced that one can live fully in His Kingdom in this life and not yet perfectly manifest the Kingdom outwardly. Sometimes men carry so heavy a load that both body and spirit are overborne. Jesus on Golgotha uttered a heart-rending cry of spiritual abandonment; Paul prayed ineffectually three times to have the "thorn" removed, only to be told, "My strength is made perfect in weakness"; he suffered spiritual anguish "like a pain that never leaves me" by the refusal of his own countrymen to accept the Gospel. Kagawa has hardly a sound organ in his body; and Livingstone, whose shattered arm never healed, had ulcers on both feet, and as an added burden, he suffered continual attacks of dysentery and malaria.

There are also those whose nervous and physical systems have been disturbed by the shocks of war, heavy labor, or prolonged malnutrition, but who are basically serene and unafraid. It is said that Nicolas Berdyaev, the great Russian theologian, had a nervous tic which made him compulsively clamp his hand over his mouth, a result perhaps of subconscious pressures to keep secret the names of men whose disclosure would have led to their torture and death. Yet he was inwardly free, creative, and full of faith. We know these ills are not willed by God, but we must trust Him to give this Kingdom in its fullness when and where He will. We may live fully in it now, leaving the final consummation in outward perfection to Him in His own time.

In response to the essential question of this chapter—Is any rebuff in prayer sufficient to warrant giving up prayer itself?—Mother Juliana of Norwich would reply, "I am sure . . . that either we abide a better time, or more grace, or a better gift." And Jesus tells us that men ought always to pray and never to lose heart.

In the light of these considerations, what should we do? Let us continue to study and experiment with the proper conditions

of prayer. Let us keep working with God in all the other multi-
form areas of co-operation with Him. And always let us in all
simplicity pray about everything, leaving aside our doubts while
we pray.

> For us there is only the trying,
> The rest is not our business.

Our responsibility is to pray and to leave the results to God.
"The privilege of prayer to me," testifies Grenfell of Labrador,
"is one of the most cherished possessions, because faith and experience alike convince me that God himself sees and answers,
and His answers I never venture to criticise. It is only my part
to ask. If it were otherwise I would not dare to pray at all."

CHAPTER 4

The Spectrum

of Prayer

"Life," writes the poet Shelley, "like a dome of many colored glass, stains the white radiance of eternity." Authentic prayer, like white sunlight, is one, but when this light is put through a prism, it is shattered into the rainbow of the spectrum. If we analyze God's radiant presence in the prism of our understanding, we scatter it into the many moods and types of prayer, each a colorful fragment of the whole. Though prayer is indeed not many things, like adoration, confession, and petition, but the simple immediacy of God in the soul, nevertheless, to aid our understanding and to improve our practice we may study these many moods, their meanings and patterns, all the way from the infrared of adoration to the ultraviolet of communion.

Through centuries of experience, discipline, and reflection, an over-all pattern of Christian prayer has emerged. Both the logical and psychological sequences of prayer have been established. Each part develops from and reaffirms its predecessor:

The incentive for prayer (arising from life situations)
Preparation for prayer (including mental prayer)

Adoration

Confession

Petition (general, intercession, problem-solving, and guidance)

Commitment

Thanksgiving

Communion

The practice of the Presence of God.

We pray because we are in need. Our dull consciousness seems content to feed, reproduce, and sleep unless we are needled into awareness by some barrier to immediate physical satisfaction. This is the lowly beginning of our spiritual development. The philosopher John Dewey points out that even science and philosophy have their origins in the painful stimulation of some problem. We need not rebel at such beginnings. In fact, there is some reassurance in a humble starting point of prayer. No one need protest that he is not yet advanced enough to pray. Out of our illnesses and anxieties, our social and political failures, our wars and famines, will arise the stimuli for great prayer. Arnold Toynbee writes of the "stimulus of hard countries" in the origins of civilization and socal inventiveness; we could write of the stimulus of hard circumstances in the origin of the spiritual life.

One of the most instructive Biblical passages on prayer is the description of the vision of Isaiah of Jerusalem in 740 B.C. The time of his ecstasy was "the year that King Uzziah died," a time of social crisis following a long and corrupt reign by a leprous king. In great perplexity Isaiah must have gone into the Temple to seek the wisdom of the Lord. We are not told how he prepared himself for what was to come, but we may presume that the fullness did not flash upon him without some time of waiting and watching.

The great experience begins in adoration, "I saw the Lord high and lifted up and his train filling the Temple," and the heavenly beings sang, "Holy, Holy, Holy, Lord God of Hosts. All the earth is full of thy glory." How long the prophet lay wrapped in awed wonder at the "sight" of the universal King we do not know, but the response of his wonder at the holiness of God is contrition because of his own misery and sin. "I am a man of unclean lips, and I live among a people of unclean lips, for my eyes have seen ethe glory of the Lord." The confession closes with the purging and forgiveness of God.

But Isaiah had not forgotten that he was driven to the Temple by the chaos of the time, the waywardness of the people, the need for direction and leadership. This prayer was answered by the commission of the prophet to speak the words of truth to the nation. The call of the Lord emerged out of the prayer for the people, and Isaiah responded, "Here am I, send me."

We have to complete the details with our own imaginative understanding, but it does not seem improbable that the prophet remained to thank God for the unexpected and overwhelming response to his need, and that, as he meditated on the mystery of this encounter, he felt the One who had been so high and lifted up now as near to him as the beating of his own heart. If we need proof of his certainty of the indwelling power, we have only to look at the career he pursued through the most disconcerting events of his time. If we accept the tradition of his death, we may presume that this same power sustained him even when Manasseh's torturers sawed his body into pieces.

This living experience exhibits the pattern we are to study.

The illustration is taken from the Old Testament, but the central principle underlying our understanding is from the New Testament. Our starting point is God as the Holy, Creative Love revealed in the person of Jesus Christ our Lord. Even when material comes from many sources, Christ is the light in which it is interpreted. The Christian approach to prayer will determine both what is said of the meaning of each type of prayer and the suggestions for its practice. All the truth about the spiritual life belongs to Christ. He is the key to what has preceded and what follows. With him as guide we may safely draw from all the lore of the non-Christian faiths, from philosophy, from modern science, and from any and all experiences which the human race has reported in its devious religious groping and grasping.

ON STUDYING AND PRACTICING PRAYER

The evangelical tradition of spontaneous religious devotion will seem opposed to what appears to be a cold-blooded study and exercise in prayer, but the opposition is merely apparent. The evangelical spirit should underlie all "works of prayer." Prayer is a gift of God and a work of His grace. Our study and practice must be rooted in that awareness. He inspires us, He draws us out, He gives us the gift of prayer; but He may also call us to discipline, study, and hard labor in prayer as well. St. Paul wrote, "Work out your own salvation with fear and trembling. For it is God which worketh in you both to will and to do. . . ." Here is no slackness or laziness of spirit, but at the same time no basis for a merit system of pride in spiritual works.

A total dependence upon Grace in prayer is no excuse for an undisciplined life. Such disorder, indeed, may be a sign that the gift of grace is not present. Surely this most important action of our lives should not compare unfavorably with secular activities. Circus acrobatics, for example, are often truly remarkable. A man stands on a slack rope and throws a half a dozen cups and saucers onto his head from the toe of his right foot. Such discipline on behalf of a circus crowd! How poorly our awkward and undisciplined prayer life compares with what men will do for the applause of an audience.

Although prayer is not essentially discipline nor effort, the greatest saints have never neglected either of them. A master of Zen states their strange relationship. "In the Tao [The Way of

Heaven]," writes Ma-tsu, "there is nothing to discipline onself in. If there is any discipline in it, the completion of such discipline means the destruction of the Tao [the spiritual life]. . . . But if there is no discipline whatever in the Tao, one remains an ignoramus."

The evangelical spirit, as contrasted to the grim mastery of technique or to the thought that prayer is chiefly a human effort, transforms all devotion. *Confession*, for example, becomes a joyful shedding of evil rather than active resistance, letting the light shine rather than beating at the darkness. Augustine's paradoxical cry to God for continence, "Grant what thou commandest, and command what thou willest," becomes a true description of the praying soul.

All forms of *petition*, transformed by the consciousness of God's gift of grace, become phases of the joyful receiving of the Kingdom which God is always pressing upon us. The intense moral earnestness of the prophetic longing to draw God into and thereby transform the world, is changed into grateful acceptance by the promise of Jesus, "It is your Father's good pleasure to give you the kingdom." In this new spirit the prophetic transformation of worldly existence continues apace, and the creative work of God is released through our labors of faith, hope, and love. The prayer of *communion*, often interpreted as a high human achievement, becomes instead thanksgiving for His incarnational unity with us through grace. We come to realize that nothing we do can bring God nearer nor can remove us from His Presence. As the Psalmist says, "If I ascend to heaven, thou art there! If I make my bed in Sheol, thou art there!" Thus the prayer of *Union* becomes a holy desire to express appropriately in attitude and act the given fact of that Presence.

When we understand the spirit underlying study and discipline, we realize that many good things are added by such efforts. First, the life of prayer is stabilized and steadied. In the *Four Quartets*, T. S. Eliot writes of the "moment in the rose garden, the moment in the draughty church at smoke-fall . . . lost in a shaft of sunlight . . . or the winter lightning or the waterfall." Of such moments he says, "I can only say, there we have been: but I cannot say where. And I cannot say, how long, for that is to place it in time . . . I can only say, there we have been: but I cannot say where . . . beyond any meaning we assign to happiness." But he adds,

> These are only hints and guesses,
> Hints followed by guesses; and the rest
> Is prayer, observance, discipline, thought and action.

Through disciplined prayer these luminous "moments" become more frequent and pervasive, until at last they are knit into a continuous life of adoration. The spiritual life, like the life of love, needs to go on from being honey and wine to become the daily nourishment of bread and meat.

The prayer life, furthermore, grows richer through discipline. It increases its range by venturing into types of prayer to which one might not be ordinarily drawn by temperament or station in life. This effort naturally leads to sharing with others. Such an exchange makes possible a mastery denied to the devotee of spontaneous devotion. Years ago Henry Nelson Wieman pleaded for an exchange of methods in prayer which would lead to greater proficiency. He observed that before men had exchanged detailed knowledge of swimming techniques, no one was able to swim the English Channel, a feat which has now become commonplace. "What is needed," writes the English psychoanalyst Geraldine Coster, "is a new kind of Society for Psychical Research which will concern itself with the production of genuinely supernatural phenomena in this life."

Finally, the spiritual life is not to be found at the end of a long set of spiritual exercises and disciplines; it comes at the very beginning. Do not look for the Kingdom afar off; it is "within you." Every step of the pilgrimage is accompanied by the One who initiated the journey. Each stage has its own realization and is actually the Kingdom in embryo. Jesus said, "If I by the finger of God cast out devils, no doubt the kingdom of God is come upon you." Each moment of spiritual power is a manifestation of the Kingdom. Anxiety and hurry in prayer lead to frustration. There is no point in rushing through many exercises and methods. The seed, stalk, blossom, and fruit has each a beauty and a meaning of its own.

In the pages which follow, each hue in the spectrum of prayer will pass before us in turn. Each will add its own color to the devotional life, conveying meanings peculiar to its own nature and demanding practices appropriate to its own purposes.

CHAPTER 5

The Starting Point:

God Is God

"Thine, O Lord, is the greatness, and the power, and the glory, and the victory, and the majesty; for all that is in the heavens and in the earth is thine; thine is the kingdom, O Lord, and thou art exalted as head above all." With these words King David consecrated the treasures collected for the building of the great Temple and clearly set forth the theocentric focus of all true prayer and worship.

Our uneasiness and concern over things as they are may provide a stimulus to search for some outside help, but God and His Will, His Glory, His Holiness, and His Majesty must provide the center and frame of all our praying. Evelyn Underhill writes of "the upward and outward look of humble and joyful admiration." Continuing, she speaks of "awestruck delight in the splendour and beauty of God . . . in and for Himself alone, as the very colour of life; giving its quality of unearthly beauty to the harshest, most disconcerting forms and the dreariest stretches of experience. *This is adoration: not a difficult religious exercise,*

but an attitude of the soul. . . . What a contrast this almost in-
articulate act of measureless adoration is to what Karl Barth calls
the dreadful prattle of theology: 'Hallowed be Thy Name' . . .
Before that Name let the most soaring intellects cover their
eyes with their wings and adore. Compared with this, even the
coming of the Kingdom and the doing of the Will are side issues;
articular demonstrations of the Majesty of the Infinite God, on
whom all centers, and for whom all is done." Nothing else we say
of prayer must contradict this concept of God, "High and lifted
up," and those more intimate and personal descriptions of God's
work must ever be seen against this background of sheer awesome
majesty.

Not long ago our family enjoyed a summer holiday on an
Oregon beach. The beautiful, and always troubled ocean continuously poured great restless waves upon the long stretches of
sand. The signs made clear that it would be dangerous to swim
except when the tide was coming in, and we obeyed them. But
many times as we walked into the ocean, I saw my wife and
children disappear beneath the foam of a breaker. Each time my
heart felt fear. I thought of the depths from which the ocean's
power flowed and of the weakness of the most powerful swimmer
against those mighty crashing forces. This sea, I reminded myself,
could at any time sweep adult or child to watery death. I thought
often of the Psalm:

> The Eternal is reigning, robed in majesty;
>   the Eternal is robed with a girdle of power.
> . . . .
> The floods may storm, O thou Eternal,
>   the floods may storm aloud,
>   the floods may storm and thunder;
> But high above the roaring billows,
>   high above the ocean breakers,
>   the Eternal stands supreme.

Is it not true that our praying has been directed largely to some other being than the Lord of the whole universe? Anthropologists report that every primitive people believe not only in their local and intimate deities who control crops, fertility, success in fishing and hunting, but also in a "high god" who is often said to have made everything that is. But—and in this we are like them—they do not pray nor offer sacrifices to the "high god." He is too vast and remote. All their religious traffic is carried on with the lesser deities whom they can control to some extent. Throughout much of the Old Testament the prophets are portrayed as struggling with this inveterate tendency of the people to turn their back upon God and worship the more intimate and comforting figments of their imagination who have been fashioned into images by their own hands.

God, as Rudolph Otto says, is always *"Mysterium Tremendum."* In his misery Job clamors to debate his case with God, but when in the whirlwind he is overshadowed by the majesty of the Eternal, he cries, "I am of small account; what shall I answer thee? I lay my hand on my mouth." And when the vision of the Eternal is complete, Job cries again, "I have uttered what I did not understand, things too wonderful for me, which I did not know. . . . I had heard of thee by the hearing of the ear, but now my eye sees thee; therefore I despise myself, and repent in dust and ashes."

The philosopher T. V. Smith thinks Job gave up too soon and that he should have insisted upon an answer to the problem of evil. He does not seem to appreciate the fact that man cannot discuss philosophy with God nor call Him to account, or that both man's reason and standards of moral judgment are derived from the very source which he would thus challenge. The Book of Job is not a philosophical answer to the problem of evil; it is a description of man's proper creaturely relation to God.

The experience of Job is not unique. The best-beloved scripture of Hinduism, *The Bhagavad Gita,* describes a similar over-shadowing of man by the majesty of God. Arjuna, the great warrior, speaks to his charioteer who is Brahman [God] disguised in human form, and says, "I long to behold your divine Form." Krishna replies, "O conqueror of sloth, this very day you shall behold the whole universe with all things animate and inert made one within this body of mine."

The story continues: "When he had spoken these words, Sri Krishna . . . revealed to Arjuna his transcendent form, speaking from innumerable mouths, seeing with myriad eyes, of many marvellous aspects, adorned with countless divine ornaments, brandishing all kinds of heavenly weapons, wearing celestial gar-lands and the raiment of paradise, anointed with perfumes of heavenly fragrance, full of revelations, resplendent, boundless, of ubiquitous regard.

"Suppose a thousand suns should rise together into the sky: such is the glory of the Shape of Infinite God.

"Then the son of Pandu [Arjuna] beheld the entire universe, in all its multitudinous diversity, lodged as one being within the body of the God of gods.

"Then was Arjuna, that lord of mighty riches, overcome with wonder. His hair stood erect. He bowed low before God in adora-tion, and clasped his hands and spoke, . . .

"Author of this world, the unmoved and the moving, You alone are fit for worship, you the highest. Where in the three worlds shall any find your equal, Therefore I bow down, prostrate, and ask for pardon: Now forgive me, God, as friend forgives his comrade, Father forgives son, and man his dearest lover. I have seen what no man ever saw before me: Deep is my delight, but still my dread is greater."

The mystery of God can never be elucidated, for He is "That before whom words recoil." The Chinese mystic says: "The Tao that can be spoken is not the Tao. If a man should attempt to

speak of it he would be greeted with loud laughter." God is not
an object of thought but our "ultimate and intimate concern,"
the focus of all those ultimate judgments about fact and value
which bear intimately on every phase of our very existence. In
prayer we come into the presence of One who is over against us,
yet wholly possessing us, whom we do not clearly know, but
toward whom all our thoughts inevitably turn.

No writer has more eloquently described the fact of this surrounding mystery than the author of Psalm 139:

> Thou searchest me, Eternal One, thou knowest me,
> Thou knowest me sitting or rising,
> My very thoughts thou readest from afar;
> Walking or resting, I am scanned by thee,
> And all my life to thee lies open;
> Ere ever a word comes to my tongue, O Thou Eternal,
> 'Tis well known to thee;
> Thou art on every side, behind me and before,
> Laying thy hand on me.
> Such knowledge is too wonderful for me;
> It is far, far beyond me.
>
> Where could I go from thy Spirit,
> Where could I flee from thy face?
> I climb to heaven?—but thou art there;
> I nestle in the nether-world?—and there thou art!
> If I darted swift to the dawn,
> To the verge of ocean afar,
> Thy hand even there would fall on me,
> Thy right hand would reach me.
>
> If I say, "The dark will screen me,
> Night will hide me in its curtains,"
> Yet darkness is not dark to thee,
> The night is clear as daylight.

I praise thee for the awful wonder of my birth;
Thy work is wonderful.
For thou didst form my being,
Didst weave me in my mother's womb.
Thou knewest all about my soul,
My body was no mystery to thee,
As I was being moulded secretly
And put together in the world below;
. . . .

O God, what mysteries I find in thee!
How vast the number of thy purposes!
I try to count them?—they are more than the sand;
I wake from my reverie, and I am still lost in thee.
. . . .

Search me, O God, and know my heart,
Test me and try my thoughts;
See if I am taking a wrong course,
And do thou lead me on the lines of life eternal.

This superb prayer is a model of God's priority. Our body, mind, and soul are dependent upon Him, have been made by Him, continue in His care, and are constantly surrounded by the unsearchable vastness of His mystery. Any approach to prayer which has less than this at its center is sheer absurdity.

This psalm reverses the usual order. We imagine that we seek God, that we argue to prove His existence, and that we call Him to our aid in prayer. The opposite is true. We do not attain to Him; He contains us. We do not seek Him out; He finds us out. We do not prove Him; He proves us. Even our attempts to escape Him are futile. We attempt to disprove His existence, but we must assume His reason to support our argument; we cry out against the evil of the world in denial of His love and power, but it is His tendering of our conscience which makes us sensitive to the evil which He too opposes; we moan against the meaninglessness of existence, but again we must have a clue to mean-

E

ing in order to grasp the sense of our own argument. If we hatefully seek to destroy in His world, we must use His reason to plot our acts, His love to form our band, His integrity to bind them to secrecy. And from the first, as the psychologists are now saying, it is our desire to be loved and our fear of rejection by our fellow beings which makes us at once so defiant and so pitiable. The great apostle has written, "There is . . . one God and Father of us all, who is above all and through all, and in all." There is no escape, and those who know Him rejoice with fear and trembling that this is so.

In our egotism, making his purposes too parochial and too easily comprehended, we forget that beyond the "observable universe" are mysteries we can never grasp. If God be God, this must be so! We need not share the fear of Logan Pearsall Smith who wrote: "I am sometimes afraid of finding that there is a moral for everything; that the whole great frame of the Universe has a key, like a box; has been contrived and set going by a well-meaning but humdrum Eighteenth-century Creator. It would be a kind of Hell, surely, a world in which everything could be at once explained, shown to be obvious and useful." There will always be a large place in any Christian's prayer life for a "reverent agnosticism," the *via negativa,* the approach which recognizes that all our assertions about Deity are partial and fragmentary and hence not literally true, and which therefore says of all such positive claims, "Not quite this, not quite this, not quite this!"

The universe revealed in modern astronomy does indeed enlarge man's conception of God's creative mystery and power. New speculations, while accentuating man's smallness and nature's vastness, have brought the mystery of creation up to date. Scientists such as Coulson, Whittaker, Jordan, Bondi, Gold, and Hoyle have asserted that creation is still going on throughout all space. This hypothesis, they claim, is fundamental to a modern cosmology. Furthermore, they are prepared to say that the amount of matter which is being created (out of nothing!) within the "observable universe" (a globe roughly two billion light years' radius) *is a nonillian* (100,000,000,000,000,000,000,000,000,-000,000) tons per second. This is more matter than our entire solar system. Unimaginable as are these amounts, one thought about what lies beyond leads the mind to stark emptiness. "If you explore the life of things and of conditioned being," writes Martin Buber, "you come to the unfathomable."

The quality of our experience in adoration is the "giveness" of God, His "self-revelation," as the Continental theologians have been at such pains to make clear. He is the eternal Subject over against us, Berdyaev argues, never an Object for our thought. The world of objects is merely a symbol world for our discussions, an abstraction from the living world of God. "God cannot be inferred in anything—in nature, say, as its author, or in history as its master, or in the subject as the self that is thought in it," writes Martin Buber. "Something else is not 'given' and then God elicited from it; but God is the Being that is directly, most nearly, and lastingly, over against us, that may be only addressed, not expressed."

This quality of adoration can save us from many frightful errors in prayer. Modern devotion has become entangled in two perverse developments, "peace of mind religion" and "culture religion." In the first, prayer becomes a technique for healing the body or mind, for guaranteeing success in the accumulation of wealth, or for the allaying of anxieties and physical disabilities. It is natural for people to turn to any promising technique to meet their economic, physical, and psychological needs, and prayer contains the essence of such technique. Hence the enormous sale of books which promise such instruction.

"Culture religion" is an ancient perversion. In the eighth century before Christ, Amos, the first of the literary prophets, attacked the religiosity of his day primarily for measuring God in cultural terms. The "chosen people" psychology appears almost without fail in each new nation. It becomes overwhelmingly easy to equate God's will with the way men do things. Then they imagine that their security and success must be His primary concern.

Prayer normally produces health and peace of mind and, furthermore, tends to make a people vigorous and creative along the lines of their own special genius, but when either of these natural goods becomes the center of devotion or the major religious appeal, man and nations, as the prophets have warned, take the well-traveled road to ultimate disillusionment. The practice of adoration—looking to God in and for Himself, losing oneself in His majesty and the beauty of His holiness—sets religion in its proper and saving focus.

Opposite to "peace of mind" or "culture religion" is the Continental theology which has sought to exalt the glory of God and His transcendent majesty by casting down man as a miserable and degraded being who cannot hope to share anything of the divine nature. This conclusion is palpably in contradiction to the significance of both Creation and Incarnation. We do not honor God by insulting Him in His works. Charles Raven rightly observes that such a theology is the product of a pathological social situation, born of decay and despair.

However we may think of God's glory, we must not think of Him in such a way as to cancel out the entire natural life with its needs and dynamic qualities of change. Nor must we, by narrowly limiting all of our knowledge of God to the Bible, depreciate man's ability to respond to other intimations of His presence, thus rejecting nature and experience as channels of revelation.

While appreciating the religious motives which prompt these conclusions, we must retort with St. Paul, "We have not so

learned Christ." He is the true interpreter of the Glory of which
we have so inadequately written. In him we find that the proper
life of prayer is "not to renounce the world, but to establish it on
its true basis."

The practice of adoration also gives depth to all the other
moods of prayer. "The marks of revelation—mystery, miracle,
and ecstasy," writes Paul Tillich, "—are present in every true
prayer. . . . It is the presence of the mystery of being and an
actualization of our ultimate concern. If it is brought down to
the level of a conversation (or for that matter co-operation) between two beings, it is blasphemous and ridiculous." We are led
by Jesus to dare to call God "Father" in an intimate colloquy of
the soul, and, as St. Paul noted, this intimacy is itself prompted
by the Spirit which makes us cry, "Abba." Yet we entirely miss
the meaning of this intimate communion unless it is set against
the awesome vastness of the Adorable Majesty. A chatty prayer is
essentially false. We are bidden to intimacy only by God Himself
who thus lends to our daring a humility which would otherwise
be presumptuousness. And, surely, nothing is more unreal than
to imagine we are talking with God on the same terms we may
use with our neighbor, or, to use the current expression, "the
man upstairs." The wonder of the Incarnation and the gift of the
Spirit lies in its dimension of depth. The intimate and the
ultimate, the immanent and transcendent, loving-kindness and
unlimited power, are qualities that mutually enrich one another.
Only in the wedding of these polar truths is the mystery of God's
gracious presence saved from stupid sentimentality. This does
not mean that we are to be less intimate, but rather that we are
to know this intimacy against the background of ultimacy. The
comforting words of the Lord's Prayer, "Our Father," are addressed to the Being who warned, "There shall no man see me
and live!"

So through the whole range of prayer—petition, intercession, communion, and the rest—we humbly bring into His presence our need, the stuff of our world, and all our devotion becomes an act of effective adoration.

Even our creatureliness must not lead us to empty man of being and reality. "Yes; in pure relation," writes Buber, penetrating to the core of our experience, "you have felt yourself to be simply dependent, as you are able to feel in no other relation—and simply free, too, as in no other time or place: you have felt yourself to be both creaturely and creative. You had the one feeling then no longer limited by the other, but you had both of them limitlessly and together."

Then he adds this bold observation: "The man who prays pours himself out in unrestrained dependence, and knows that he has—in an incomprehensible way—an effect upon God, even though he obtains nothing from God; for when he no longer desires anything for himself he sees the flame of his effect burning at its highest. . . . This is known by him too who offers up his little will to God and meets Him in the grand will. 'Thy will be done,' he says, and says no more; but truth adds for him 'through me whom Thou needest.' "

Prayer begins in adoration. This is the starting point: God is God. However, He is not only the transcendent God; He is the loving Word spoken through Jesus as the Christ. We are called beyond adoration. He leads us into the mystery of other dimensions of prayer.

CHAPTER 6

The Meaning

of Confession

The prayer of adoration, looking toward the holiness of God, initiates a reflex by which we see ourselves in an entirely new light. This light discloses our own emptiness and fragmentariness, and our distance from the person we might be in and for God. Thus adoration leads to confession.

The purpose of confession is to turn us from ourselves to God, from our neurotic satisfaction with sham selfhood to true maturity, and from selfish sensual preoccupation to love of our fellows. Is not this to learn to love God with our heart, soul, mind, and strength, and our neighbor as ourselves? Is it not also to turn from the unreal to the Real?

CONFESSION AS TURNING TOWARD REALITY

Confession begins when a man stands before the holy, mysterious, yet loving God who says, "Be holy, for I am holy," a command reaffirmed by Jesus, "Be perfect, as your heavenly Father is perfect." Our self-enclosure is broken through by the supremely Real, and our prayer, now stirred to fresh life, is that we be set in true relation to all Reality, to our fellows, to ourselves, and to the world we call nature. At such moments we realize that most of our life has been spent in the building of a self-enclosing prison which has gradually alienated us from the life around us. Evelyn Underhill has written: "By false desires and false thoughts man has built up for himself a false universe: as a mollusk, by the deliberate and persistent absorption of lime and rejection of all else, can build up for itself a hard shell which shuts it from the external world, and only represents in a distorted and unrecognizable form the ocean from which it was obtained. This hard and wholly unnutritious shell, this one-sided secretion of the surface consciousness, makes as it were a little cave of illusion for each separate soul."

Confessional prayer is the continuous opening of our small selves to the influence of God in the faith that He will dissolve these rigid ego-made prisons, these "caves of illusion," and bring us, as St. Paul says, into "the glorious liberty of His own sons." This is not a medieval or Oriental ideal of purgation—a stripping which leads us out of the world and into a "spiritual" realm— but a new relating of ourselves to all levels of existence. God is present and at work in everything. This is His world, we are His people, and history is His providence. This is hard to believe because we have been too self-absorbed to see Reality as it is. When the inner spirit is no longer curved back upon itself, then all the old commonplace facts shine with a new luminosity. As a Zen Master said:

> How wondrously supernatural.
> And how miraculous, this!
> I draw water, and I carry fuel.

Two alternative orientations or philosophies of life lie open for every man. One centers on Reality; the other centers on the ego. The ego is not the true self, but a false picture which we confuse with our true selves. It is a conglomerate image which has been built out of neurotic hopes and illusions, the expectations of our fellows, the roles which we are required to play in the social scheme, and other forces of which we must become aware in the enterprise of spiritual liberation.

Despite the fact that the ego is a sham center, a distorted, shallow, and rigid caricature of our true self, it is prized above all other things and made the center of all existence. Everything is evaluated in terms of it. By contrast, Reality is the totality of Life Fact which both lies over against ourselves and surges within as our true self, and which is continuously either teasing us or tormenting us to leave our "cave of illusion" where the ego sits enthroned. Our real life and selfhood lies in orienting ourselves to this Reality, but this requires more courage, faith, and love than we possess.

Fortunately, the effort of the ego to maintain its central position is bound to fail, but the pain and loss suffered in the struggle are appalling, and at times nearly all our energies are channeled into such futile work. Even prayer is drafted for this service, but prayer is dangerous to the ego, because God is the center of Reality—He is Reality—and to traffic with Him even on behalf of the ego is to endanger its supremacy. Of necessity the ego is afraid, hostile, proud, deceitful, greedy, and at the same time guilty and inferior, for it perceives the world as a threat, while at the same time in the depths of its own being it knows the total goodness of the Reality. The poet Tagore expresses this tragic dualism:

> I came out alone on my way to my tryst. But who is this
>   that follows me in the silent dark?
> I move aside to avoid his presence, but I escape him not.
> He makes the dust rise from the earth with his swagger;
>   he adds his loud voice to every word that I utter.
> He is my own little self, my lord, he knows no shame; but
>   I am ashamed to come to thy door in his company.

The contrast of reality-and-ego orientation can be best seen when a person finds the ongoing course of his life interrupted by a perplexing problem and its attendant discomforts and tensions. The ego immediately concerns itself with reducing the discomfort and tension and returning to the previous habitual state. The reality-oriented self accepts the stimulation and challenge of the intrusion, and using the inward tensions as a stimulus to effort and thought, concentrates attention upon resolving the problematic situation which has arisen. The power of problems to reveal our ultimate life orientation is due to the fact that crucial life situations are as complex as reality itself and demand of us a total responsiveness. An authentic problem requires not merely attention to facts as the realist insists, but also imaginative sympathy with the persons involved, a power to discriminate the relevant values, and, finally, a kind of prophetic intuition of the genuine possibilities in the whole setting.

The ego-oriented individual is not able to be sensitive to the multidimensional reality which lies within and beyond him. He is absorbed in restoring the ego to its position of unruffled comfort and composure. Thus a problem arouses in him anger or fear, and his resourcefulness is spent in finding some punishment for the intruder or some escape from its influences. The remarkable ingenuity of the ego in building pseudo-solutions has supplied abnormal psychologists ample field for study. Their conclusions are of great value in routing the ego from its hiding places and allowing God to dissolve this shadow with a shaft of His own healing light.

Confession as reality-orientation is a recognition of the sovereign obligation and saving power of truth. Practice of such confession is the habitual prayer to God that He will dig us out of our burrows and rebuild our inner energies so that we may live with Him in His world. This much truth can do, but at the core of our resistance to truth is our failure to love.

CONFESSION AS LEARNING TO LOVE

Confession may thus be interpreted as a longing to let the love of God rule every moment of existence. "Love. . . !" says our Lord. Upon this "depend all the law and the prophets." In addition, his life, the manner of his death, and the mystery of his resurrection are all commentaries on the true meaning of love itself. Through him the golden rule becomes loving one another as he has loved us. He also makes plausible St. John's bold words, "He that dwelleth in love dwelleth in God and God in him."

Our Lord's earthly ministry reveals the diverse dimensions of divine love. At first in Galilee the ministry is hopeful, buoyant, and expectant. The wonders of the Kingdom are announced and men press rapidly into it. Healings, conversions, and deep fellowship abound as men see glimpses of what it might be like if they responded freely to the love of God. Perhaps the glorious Kingdom will come before the evangelists can visit all the cities of Israel!

The Judean ministry reveals an even greater depth of faith and love, for it shows Jesus in the face of raging hate and cynical rejection. There the path is narrower. Joy and peace must be drawn from ultimate depths, for surface events prove tragic and love seems defeated. But the Cross is not essentially different from the lilies of the field. Both are signs of the wonder and power of creative love. The Passion reveals the resourcefulness of the divine love in the face of the barbarity of human rejection. This cross, as St. Paul saw, is a stumbling block to all who think of God's Kingdom as a triumph of open power, but to those who live within the love so revealed it is the power of God unto salvation. It is the continual price paid for redemptive activity and is the creative work of love in the face of human rejection. "We are still a long way from appreciating the significance of our emblem," Charles Raven reminds us, "seeing in suffering the basic quality of the creative, redemptive and sanctifying process,

> "That only black Gethsemane can prove
> The pain, the triumph and the peace of love."

The picture of God revealed by Jesus is fundamental for prayer. He is the supreme Being who responds in love to every living event of the universe. As Charles Hartshorne says, "To say that Jesus was God, then, ought to mean that God Himself is one with us in our suffering, that divine love is not essentially benevolence—external well-wishing—but sympathy, taking into itself our very grief." William Blake wrote:

> Oh, he gives to us his joy
> That our grief he may destroy;
> Till our grief is fled and gone
> He doth sit by us and moan.

C. S. Lewis' essay on "Pain" contains the comforting assurance that pain cannot be added; the total amount of pain in the world could not be your pain plus mine, plus every other person's, because there would be no being to suffer that cumulative pain. The maximum pain in the world is whatever one person alone can experience. For those who have felt pain to the limit of consciousness and known in those flashing moments that it is still endurable, this consideration does seem to mitigate the problem of suffering.

Unfortunately, in my opinion, this view of private pain unshared throughout the universe is not true.

If God is love, then He is the Being who perceives the feelings of the entire universe, a universe which must now be thought of as alive throughout and in continuous process and growth, a growth which induces the "agonizing longing" noted by St. Paul. He is the being who sympathetically includes it all, enjoys it all, and suffers it all. In short, there is a Person to whom the sum total of suffering is immediately experienced. How humbling and overwhelming this is. And to begin to realize it in even the slightest degree calls the soul out of its selfishness to new dimensions of awareness.

What are some of the direct consequences for prayer in such a conception of Reality? Prayer becomes the joyful sharing of the pain of all existence and a longing to participate in its eradication. Prayer becomes an enlarging sympathy for all selves until the cosmic Self in all its richness becomes the ultimate frame of reference in every attitude and action. Prayer becomes faith in action—deciding, running risks, shaping indeterminate events, creating within the highest frame of possibilities. Prayer becomes trust that the ultimate Self loves and is able to sustain all values, wherever they appear, and, therefore, can be entrusted with the whole of life and its dearest concerns. There comes the realization that nothing valuable is lost and an intense longing to add to that value in some way. There comes, too, a refusal to add to the suffering of the ultimate Person. In prayer we feel the presence of all the events in the world and we long for their highest welfare. We "love them as God loves them." Prayer gives the recognition that there is no ultimate separateness, but rather a unity in love in which individuality, far from being lost in bare oneness, is enhanced, prized, and developed to its highest possibility. And, finally, since love is the power which moves the world, loving intercession—focusing expectant love on another person— opens for man the means to actualize his highest potentiality.

Turning to the classic description of the Christian life, the Sermon on the Mount, we find again that the key is love. With supreme genius Jesus surgically exposes those hidden attitudes which are at the center of our resistance to God. Each example reveals one more phase of our refusal to enter into mutuality with one another and into loving trust toward God: *Anger,* contempt—the will to exclude another from the common share of good; *deceit*—the erection of barriers to genuine encounter, the will to manipulate another person as a thing by force rather than persuade by the truth; *lust*—the will to exploit another sexually, to treat a human being as a mere toy of pleasure rather than as a person; *pride*—the temptation of the "good" man who fasts, prays, and gives to charity, the will to regard myself as the owner of goodness, the possessor of virtues, and to exclude as "bad" men those who do not fit my patterns of expectation; *greed*—the will to find security in physical wealth instead of in God, even at the expense of the welfare of my fellow human beings; *hypocrisy*—the use of the appearance of goodness to excuse me from entering into direct relationship with my fellows; *anxiety*—a fundamental distrust of the love of God, the facing of life fearfully, not expectantly; criticism, *judging*—a device by which, cutting my rivals down to size, I make my status and prestige, not mutual aid and affection, the goal; *busyness*, doing many good works "in my Name," but, lost in a whirl of socially approved acts, I avoid real encounters with living persons.

During recent decades the New Testament teaching on Love has received confirmation from scholars in many fields as they amass more and more evidence for love as the fundamental factor in human welfare.

Biologists have begun to modify the Darwinian picture of nature as "red in tooth and claw." Violence and cunning are seen as the by-products of a fatal specialization which gives a momentary advantage in fight or flight but prevents further development. The violence of the animal world is due to its having turned into a blind alley. The evolutionary future has always belonged to the curious, sensitive, emotionally vivid, physically flexible, and co-operative species. Mutual aid and intelligence are more nearly the key to nature's law. Man alone among the

higher mammals seems to have avoided the irreversible development into hardness and specialization, though he seems at present
to be in danger of also moving into that blind alley.

Psychologists and other social scientists are gradually outgrow-
ing the old egoistic pleasure-pain (body-centered) theories and
are recognizing that man is essentially social. Unloved babies,
though given perfect physical care, waste away and die. Mentally
sick persons without love grow steadily worse. "To inhibit or
prevent the expression of love," writes Ashley Montagu, of the
New School for Social Research, "is to do violence to the needs,
to the structure, and to the functioning of the organism. To love
and to be loved is as necessary to the organism as the breathing
of air." The measure of human maturity is, in Leo Beck's words,
"to give and receive love freely, without guilt." Charles Hartshorne writes: "Theologians and philosophers might well join
with Menninger in longing for the day when, as he says, 'We
shall have accorded to love that pre-eminence which it deserves
in our scale of values; we shall seek it and proclaim it as the
highest virtue and the greatest boon. . . . Love is the medicine
for the sickness of the world, a prescription often given, too
rarely taken."

"Now we know from the study of overprotected children, as
also from the study of children who have had all the purely
physical needs satisfied," writes Ashley Montagu, "that the satisfaction of physical needs alone is not enough, for the greatest of
all needs of the human being is the need for love, the experienc-
ing of the feeling conveyed by 'others' that one is wanted,
needed, liked, appreciated, valued, and deeply involved with
the 'other' or 'others.'"

·Even the parapsychologists have experimentally discovered,
according to Gardner Murphy of the Menninger Clinic, that
people with ties of blood or affection show up higher in telepathy
tests than do strangers.

Sociologists, too, have developed interpretations of social life in terms of primary group values, consensus on common interests, and the importance to the individual of a meaningful share in the human group. Some scholars have even gone so far as to say that the social crisis of our age is best interpreted in terms of the human search for meaningful community, the sociological equivalent of love. In his presidential address before the Pacific Division of the American Philosophical Association in December, 1953, Melvin Rader, a distinguished social philosopher, warned, "Modern dictatorships have sought to prevent social disintegration by extreme coercion, leader-worship, and chauvinism. But the cure is worse than the disease. The alternative to both a communist or fascist dictatorship and an individualistic system of devil-take-the-hindmost is the cultivation of free, co-operative communities. Indeed, the development of co-operative ways of living to replace the present competitive ways is the prime need of mankind at this critical juncture of history." In an extended analysis of the problems bearing on the *Reconstruction of Humanity*, P. A. Sorokin of Harvard, after reviewing many social factors, concludes: "It should now be quite clear that none of the foregoing plans can assure peace. Taken alone, they are either fallacious or inadequate. Their principal defect is that they either neglect the decisive factor of altruism and love, without which war cannot be eliminated, or are unable to make the overt behavior of persons and groups, with their social and cultural institutions, more altruistic than they are now. Whatever the other prerequisites of a creative and lasting peace may be, it cannot be achieved without a substantial increase of love, sympathy, and free co-operation in the overt relationships of persons and groups."

Aldous Huxley sums up our social and personal difficulties as the product of "organized lovelessness." Toward nature, we have thought of the earth as a treasure to be exploited. Toward art, we have "effectively killed all the fundamental or useful arts and set up various kinds of mass production by machines in their place." Human beings have been considered as mere "hands" or "cogs" in our mass production. All the "organized lovelessness" which follows from mass organization in economics, business, and government climaxes in the "crowning super-structure of uncharity," the relations between state and sovereign state. There is little wonder that Lewis Mumford, who has wrestled for years with the problems of a creative reconstruction of our civilization, should, in his latest work, summarize: "The only final safeguard against the genocidal and suicidal impulses our weapons of extermination have encouraged is the sedulous devotion to love in all its aspects, beginning with tenderness. . . . The Sermon on the Mount has become the new Mount Everest that calls forth the human spirit. Nothing less than that 'impossible ascent' remains as a practical alternative to our yielding to the destructive and inhuman forces that threaten our civilization."

In philosophy the same trend of thought can be discerned. Professor Charles Hartshorne, distinguished interpreter of the philosophy of Alfred North Whitehead, has argued brilliantly in a series of works that the key to Whitehead's organismic system—and to Reality—is to be found in the single concept, "love."

The whole temper of philosophy since Descartes has begun to change. Existentialism, secular and religious, has focused attention upon a different set of problems. Up to the present time modern philosophy has been concerned largely with the relationships between things or between a knowing mind and a thing known. The new interest is focused upon the personal ("I-Thou") relationship with its dynamic qualities of anxiety and despair; loyalty, love and trust; choice and responsibility.

In this changed atmosphere a new appreciation of love has

F

been made possible. Life is fundamentally dialogue, mutuality, decision, responsibility. Older forms of knowledge are acknowledged to be abstract and largely remote from the center of human concern. Religion, on the other hand, has become more important for thought. It is now seen as man's ultimate and intimate concern, his primary loyalty and love in life, rather than a philosophical speculation about the existence or non-existence of an "object" called "God."

Dante's beatific experience of love at the heart of existence speaks with renewed authority across the intervening centuries now that the intellectual climate of our age has made it plausible again:

> Deep within its depths I saw
> Bound by love in one volume
> All the scattered leaves of the universe.

In the convergence of these diverse explorations we can affirm that the love we invoke and that grips us in prayer is not our pathetic attempt to generate warmth in a cold and alien universe, but is the vast being of God Himself, the essential nature of existence by which we live and grow together. As we move from intellectual reflection to self-exposure to Him in confession we learn that Love does not belong to us, we belong to Him. We press forward to the time in prayer when all our resistance to this primal force is swept away and we experience for ourselves the state described in the final lines of Dante's *Paradiso*:

> . . . my volition now, and my desires,
> Were moved like a wheel revolving evenly
> By love that moves the sun and starry fires.

Confession, we have seen thus far, may be interpreted as a progressive unfolding of truth, of reality-orientation, and as growth in love. These abstract concepts are given greater significance if we translate them into yet other terms and describe con-

fession as growth, more specifically as growth into the maturity
seen in Jesus Christ.

CONFESSION AS GROWING UP TO THE MATURITY OF JESUS CHRIST

"Our ambition for you," writes St. Paul to the Corinthian
Church, "is *true Christian maturity*." This same goal is echoed
in the moving words of the Liturgy of the Holy Communion:
"That we may be filled with the fullness of his life, may grow
into his likeness and evermore dwell in him and he in us . . .
that we might become partakers of the divine nature."

This "growing up in every way unto Christ," in St. Paul's
words, is the purpose of all confessional prayer. In the words of
Keats, it is also the purpose of our whole life, for our planet is a
"vale of soul making." The totality of our life experiences is the
real school of Christ whereby God seeks to draw us into the
fullness.

Human selfhood is a great mystery. We shield ourselves from
the mystery by defining the self as a physical body, as a system
of attitudes and patterns of habits, or, perhaps, with the sociologist, as a system of socially defined roles. Each of these modes,
by interpreting the self as a thing, denies its real nature.

But the self is not an object. Consciousness always stands
"back" of any awareness of an object. It is the knower, the
Vedantists say, not the known. The relationships of selves in an
"I-Thou" pattern is entirely different from the relationship of
objects as "It-It" or even of the relationship of a self to an object
as "I-It."

The self, to be sure, is connected with its body, other selves,
the world, and God. It is not pure spirit, nor purely alone, not
even in any exact sense "simply itself." The human self is in
something beyond—in other selves, in the intricate patterns of
the world, in its own future self, in beauty, truth, goodness, and
love. Yet it never ceases to be something unique in its own right.

"The real Self," writes Fritz Kunkel, "is a goal of development rather than an immediate experience. It may be the channel through which the infinite value draws us toward the top of the pyramid of means and goals. It is impossible to have an image of our real Self—just as it is impossible to have an image of God. We are infinite like Him, and increasingly so the more we are aware of our real Selves." He goes on to say, "In the manner of popular philosophy we may call this Self the source of our most creative and most vital actions, the core of human personality; or following the unanimous tradition of the mystics: the inner light, the soul's deepest ground, the empty center of the inner universe;—but we only realize the more vividly that we do not know its true nature."

This mysterious goodness at the heart of our being is known in tragic contrast to the empirical man who is far from divine. In classic Christian experience we learn that man, disrupted, broken, and dissociated in his inward nature as he is, can be re-knit by the mercy and power of God into the greater image of the full-grown Son. In confessional prayer the fact of disruption emerges in all its ghastly dimensions, and amidst the debris of the ruined self arises a new being in Christ.

These words have meaning only to those who in genuine confession come to know their self-alienation, their contempt for others, including those whom they profess to love, their distaste for nature, and their neglect or abuse of God. Renewal is also a fact of experience. The deeper the rent which is uncovered, the profounder is the merciful power which works to heal it.

Underlying our understanding of this experience of the re-creating and sanctifying presence of God in confessional prayer is the Incarnation, God united to man in Jesus Christ. The council of Chalcedon used the formula: truly God and truly man. Christian prayer goes forward in the faith that this joining of the human and the divine has been accomplished.

What is often overlooked—and what claims our attention

here—is that the mystery of incarnation takes place in prayer. The doctrine of the Incarnation is not merely a belief touching the nature of Jesus Christ, it is an account of what takes place in the devout at the moment of true faith. According to the New Testament, the union of the human and the divine would be repeated in the life of every believer. "As many as received him, to them gave he power to become sons of God, even to them that believe on his name."

St. Paul most clearly describes this "Christing" of souls. The divine *Logos* made flesh, the Christ by whom "all things were created," is also the goal of human development. St. Paul urged "growing up in every way unto Christ," which meant for him that the very life of God which was in Jesus was to be born in his followers. This is the way he described his own experience: "Every day I die," he wrote to the Corinthian Church. And in another letter he added, "Nevertheless I live; yet not I, but Christ liveth in me."

Apart from the record of Christian experience this would seem a wild extravagance, but the promise is there in the New Testament, and the testimony of the saints to its truth is eloquent. The purpose of confessional prayer is to let Christ, the incarnating power of God, become the inner reality of our life. Jesus is the first-born of the new creation, and our elder brother. We are to follow him into the Kingdom, for "he hath given us his Spirit whereby we cry, 'Abba! Father!'"

Each of these dimensions of confession—turning toward Reality, learning to love, and growing up to the maturity of Christ— is a symbol of the same truth. Each is an intimation of the mystery of the true being which we have in God, the meaning of our life which we accept in faith even when it is hidden from us. Confessional prayer will not remove the mystery, but it will unfold it in totally unexpected and wonderful ways. To the practice of this kind of prayer we now turn.

CHAPTER 7

The Method

of Confession

If you direct the attention of a one-year-old child to some object by pointing with your hand, he will look only at the pointing finger. He cannot realize that you are referring to something beyond. The methods of prayer discussed in this chapter are pointers which refer beyond themselves; they have no inherent virtue. When that to which they refer has been attained, methods may be dispensed with. What follows is a method of confessional prayer which has grown out of many experiences. As George Fox says, "This I knew experimentally."

   I. Darkness.
      Expression of our feelings fully and honestly in the Presence of God.
      Acceptance of this negative expression and refusal to rationalize it.
      Staying in prayer until illumination dawns.
  II. Light.

Turning toward the Light in contrition, trust, and loving commitment.

Acceptance of God's forgiveness, our new status, and our new freedom.

Fully accepting and committing ourselves to the actions necessary to the full expression of the insight which has come.

III. Living in the Light.

Pouring out thanksgiving for God's gracious work done in us. Engaging in *positive* meditation on the persons and situations which have been disturbing.

Acceptance of the discipline of reconditioning ourselves to the new life.

I. *Darkness*. We begin confession with a full and honest expression of feeling *in the Presence of God*. All our rage, hate, and fear can be poured out without censorship and unchecked by guilts, rationalizations, or fears. We must be what we are before the Reality which supremely *Is*. We must not judge ourselves, or think of God as judge, for this would hinder self-revelation and our chance to move beyond such negativity. Feelings, not concepts, are the clue to our inward state. Our reluctance to express them as well as our fear or even hatred of God may be expressed in this moment. But God's presence must not be forgotten, even though we may confess that we wish He were far away. Although we may pray that He punish our enemies as in the cry of the Psalmist, "Slay the wicked, O God . . . ," we must not think of Him as judging or condemning us.

The secret of confessional prayer lies in an absolutely unfettered self-revelation in the Presence. He is beyond insult or hurt, and He can never be embarrassed nor ashamed. Since He knows us more deeply than we know ourselves, we can stand spiritually naked before Him. Unfortunately, we have too often been taught that our prayers should be polite. We speak only fitting and appropriate words even using King James English! Such an approach almost guarantees that both God and our true self will remain hidden from us.

Having poured out our feelings in unhindered self-revelation, the next step is to accept the picture of ourself which has emerged. It will be shocking, but it will be true. We must humbly acknowledge before God that we are just this hating, lusting, anxious, and prideful person who has expressed all these feelings. Such acceptance will all be hard, but it will be made immensely easier if we can remember to hold to the Presence which knew it all before we spoke a word.

If we can faithfully cling to the remembrance of God throughout this fearful exercise a miracle will surely occur. It will be the miracle of a healing and supporting light which will break through the darkness. As George Fox recorded in his *Journal*, "I saw . . . that there was an ocean of darkness and death; but an infinite ocean of light and love, which flowed over the ocean of darkness." And a friend who experimented with this pattern of confessional prayer reported, "The illuminating shift did take place." The response of God, though long delayed, will surely come.

II. *Light*. When the light at last breaks over our stormy confession we will greet it with contrition, trust, and loving commitment. We may need to remember that God's mercy is as absolutely inexhaustible as it is unfathomable. We must have courage to remember, as Lewis Maclachlan says, "that the purpose of confession is not to catalogue our sins, still less is it to gaze upon them in fearful fascination, but to get rid of them. We must therefore cast them down before God, disowning and repudiating them in an act of true repentance." He further reminds us: "We cannot make ourselves righteous by any effort of our own, but God, our Maker, can fulfill His perfect will in us if we give our consent. 'He made us and not we ourselves,' and it is He who continues to make and remake us, and not we ourselves."

Contrition must lead to an acceptance of God's forgiveness and to our new status and our new freedom in his eyes. Frequently people still cling to their guilt after confession. They seem to feel that God cannot forgive to the degree of their sins, and they fail to perceive that this is distrust of God and a denial of His mercy. This may be an inverted form of pride. We need not feel forgiven; we must simply take the forgiveness offered. On a later occasion, we may feel the necessity of confessing that we have not felt forgiven, but each time we must accept as fact that God's mercy has triumphed.

The acceptance of God's forgiving mercy must be followed by appropriate acts of restitution. The willingness to rebuild what our past acts and attitudes have destroyed may be the acid test of the whole experience of forgiveness. Such restitution will not win forgiveness—that is given without price—but it may mark the acceptance of mercy with the sign of authenticity. In Hamlet, King Claudius, who has secured his throne by murder, finds that prayer has no reality as long as he remains unwilling to consider restitution for the crime. Searching for relief from guilt, he kneels to pray and raises instead an anguished cry:

> Pray can I not,
> Though inclination be as sharp as will.
> . . . .
> My fault is past. But, O! what form of prayer
> Can serve my turn? "Forgive me my foul murder?"
> That cannot be; since I am still possess'd
> Of those effects for which I did the murder,
> My crown, mine own ambition, and my queen.
> May one be pardon'd and retain the offence?

At this stage in our confession we must freely, even joyously, accept the pledge of restitution as the clearest sign of the new self which God is miraculously bringing to birth if we will that He do it.

III. *Living in the Light*. The person who has experienced this miracle of forgiveness will not, perhaps, need a reminder that he should praise God and thank Him for His mercy and the new life. Gratitude is the natural response to God for this costly gift, and its expression will help convince the deep self that we have been authentically forgiven and restored.

Now we are prepared for positive meditation and loving intercession for those situations, problems, and persons which gave rise to our confession. Later chapters will develop this method of prayer more fully, but it is important here to note that the content of the confession will determine the keynote we select for meditation. By using our imagination we shall see our old defeating situations in an entirely new way. Let the drama unfold naturally. Though this sounds like the compensatory fantasy of daydreaming, it is quite the opposite. Instead of making up for a poor adjustment to situations and persons, it is a rehearsal for the new life which has already begun in prayer. Often in that rehearsal some of the old negativity will emerge. This one may quietly offer to God with a phrase such as "Take this lingering fear (anger, guilt, inferiority feeling) along with the rest which I have freely trusted to Thee."

Geraldine Coster makes a further suggestion. Suppose vindictiveness is a problem. Analysis reveals that vindictiveness is the opposite of a genuine gentleness. Sometimes the opposite of a negative quality may be hard to discern, for these feelings come in misleading guises. Vindictiveness, for example, may be simply an expression of timidity, or of repressed guilt, or of an impossible situation that frustrates creative work. "Having determined to eliminate vindictiveness," writes Miss Coster, a man "begins by making a close study of gentleness in all the variety of its manifestations—the feeble gentleness which goes with timidity, the courteous gentleness of the well-mannered, the sublime gentleness of the saint, which is a mixture of patience, tolerance, and power held in reserve. Thus he builds up an attraction toward the new quality, and his mind tends to flow into this pattern more and more readily. He continues to deliberate daily for some minutes upon the quality, and takes every opportunity of expressing it in practice."

A bishop of the Methodist Church once told me he felt certain that the secret of whatever strength of character he and his brothers and sisters possessed could be traced to their childhood when these virtues were "prayed into them" during family prayers.

Living in the light must be more than an inward spiritual gesture of prayer and meditation. It must reach the level of practice. These practices result from prayer, but they also lend further reality to praying itself. We must immediately practice, even if in a trifling way, some aspect of the new freedom which has emerged in meditation. We must try our hand at the new virtues, the positive qualities which are the opposite of the confessed weaknesses. This will require great effort and may at first seem unnatural or even hypocritical. We may, for example, practice generosity or unselfishness without actually feeling them. We may put on a bold front even though we are inwardly fearful. If we are faithful in this, pressures will build up which will explode into new periods of confession, new illumination, and new strength. If we practice only what we spontaneously feel, we well not grow and the inner life will remain dull.

Control without prayer is impossible, and prayer without control is unreal. The "dead heave of the will," which characterizes so much of our moral experience, is replaced after much prayer by a spontaneous obedience to goodness. Such obedience becomes

a second nature which is the goal of spiritual development and
which is more natural than the ego reflexes by which we are
now dominated. "At seventy," said Confucius, "I could do as I
pleased without breaking the moral law." Nearly a thousand
years later, St. Augustine characterized Christian maturity in
the phrase, "Love and do as you please."

The saints are known for their "heroic practice of the virtues."
At first this was accomplished through sheer effort. St. Francis
believed that the turning point in his life came at the moment
when, overcoming his natural revulsion for the scabrous appearance of a beggar, he kissed the leper's feet.

We cannot wait for the moment when we feel just right before
we begin to practice courage, temperance, and justice; or faith,
hope, and love. When these things go against the grain, we can
unburden our negative feelings in confession, but we must not
slacken our practice of them. At the beginning of his beautiful
little book, *The Spirit of St. Francis de Sales,* Jean Pierre Camus
says: "I asked the Bishop of Geneva what one must do to attain
perfection. 'You must love God with all your heart,' he answered,
'and your neighbor as yourself.'

" 'I did not ask wherein perfection lies,' I rejoined, 'but how
to attain it.' 'Charity,' he said again; 'that is both means and end,
the only way by which we can reach that perfection which is in
truth, after all, but charity itself. St. Paul says, 'I will show you
a more excellent way'; and then he enlarges more fully upon
charity. It is the life of all that is good; without charity all graces
die; it is the only way to God, the only truth, the only life of
the soul; for it brings us forth from the death of sin into the life
of grace; it kindles faith and hope. Just as the soul is the life of
the body, so charity is the life of the soul.'

" 'I know all that,' I said; 'but I want to know how one is to
love God with all one's heart, and one's neighbour as oneself.'

"But again he answered, 'We must love God with all our

hearts, and our neighbour as ourselves.'

" 'I am no further than I was,' I replied; 'tell me how to acquire such love.'

" 'The best way, the shortest and easiest way of loving God with all one's heart, . . . is to love him wholly and heartily!' He would give no other answer. At last, however, the Bishop said, 'There are many besides you who want me to tell them of methods, and systems, and secret ways of becoming perfect, and I can only tell them that the sole secret is a hearty love of God, and the only way of attaining that love is by loving. You learn to speak by speaking, to study by studying, to run by running, to work by working; and just so you learn to love God and man by loving.' "

EXAMPLES OF THE PATTERN AT WORK

In the following prayer of Jeremiah, one of mankind's greatest spiritual leaders, can be seen an example of the first part of our confessional pattern, the free expression of feeling in the presence of God. These sentiments are not what we might expect from a great prophet. In their challenge of God Himself they may even appear blasphemous. But they ring with truth. They reflect with absolute honesty the prophet's deepest feelings about his mission and the unfaithfulness of man and God.

> O Lord, thou knowest;
>> remember me and visit me,
>> and take vengeance for me on my persecutors.
> In thy forbearance take me not away;
>> know that for thy sake I bear reproach.
> Thy words were found, and I ate them,
>> and thy words became to me a joy
>> and the delight of my heart;
>> for I am called by thy name,
>> O Lord, God of hosts.

> I did not sit in the company of merrymakers,
>   nor did I rejoice;
> I sat alone, because thy hand was upon me,
>   for thou hadst filled me with indignation.
> Why is my pain unceasing,
>   my wound incurable,
>   refusing to be healed?
> Wilt thou be to me like a deceitful brook,
>   like waters that fail?

Do we imagine that we have no such feelings, that we are better than the prophets, and that we only want God's will to be fulfilled? Such illusions make our prayers unreal!

The fact that we have this record of Jeremiah's struggle with God suggests another tool of confession. He may have discovered that setting down his unedited thoughts clarified his spirit more than mere speaking. Writing is superior to the spoken word in the power to objectify emotion. It is, therefore, no surprise to discover that diaries and spiritual autobiographies have been, for spiritual leaders like Augustine, Fox, or Wesley, tools of spiritual growth. Such writing must not be set down with an audience in mind. The censorship of the anticipated reader and the conscious efforts at literary effect inhibit the freedom which gives the writing its confessional value. It must be pure self-expression. Once we have made the record, we may discover in it, during more tranquil moments, clues of great importance for the self-knowledge that leads to growth.

Another example of the confessional pattern appears in Fritz Kunkel's *In Search of Maturity*. Here he advises the application of confessional meditation to all the basic relationships of life and especially in the family. "The inner way is to go back in our imagination to the earliest scenes with them which we can find, either in memory or in mere fantasy. Be a child once more, frightened to death by your father's severity, or spoiled by the sentimentality of your aunt. And at the same time be there as the adult that you are, or even wiser than you are in reality. You will feel the child's anguish and fear, or, when spoiled, his shallow smugness. At the same time the adult's resentment will rise in angry waves. You will realize an anger, unknown so far, because it was carefully repressed. Now be honest. Tell your father or your aunt who are there without being there how you feel. They have poisoned your life, murdered your creativity. The terrific power of revenge will surge up from the unconscious and flood your consciousness. You may be carried away by your 'sacred wrath'; but remember, God is still there, too." Such an experience illustrates the nature of meditation in the first pattern, that of darkness.

The second pattern, that of light, comes when the meditation continues: "Drag your father or your aunt before His tribunal. Listen to what He may tell you. He will certainly not be the White Giant (hero protector) you want Him to be. He will disappoint you. And still you may sense His smile. Then, bewildered by rage and shame, you will recognize that you are obsessed by an image, playing a role, convinced of your own righteousness, exactly as your father or your aunt were playing a role, serving an image, being convinced of their moral right. You are certainly as weak and blind as your aunt or your father have been. You are equally human, obsessed by the same collective images, caught in the same collective misery. So you may shake hands, and forgive one another."

The confession moves to the final pattern, that of living in the light. Now you realize that "you were integrated for a minute, though on a primitive level of consciousness. This regression brought you close to the center, and its creative power can catapult you wherever you want to go. You can use your new strength for constructive development. You have unearthed your buried sword: try to reforge it into a plough. And you will

see that God has forgiven you as you have forgiven your aunt
or father."

SOME AUXILIARY AIDS TO GROWTH IN CONFESSION

An earnest use of the confessional pattern may be supported
by several auxiliary aids. One of these is the reading of books
which speak to our condition. Most of the classics of the devotional life are now available in inexpensive editions. The reading
here proposed, however, is not limited to religious books. Any
fine written work represents a man's attempt to assess his experience and to make some meaning out of his world. This is as
true of great fiction such as Dostoevski's *Brothers Karamazov*
and Tolstoy's *War and Peace* or works of psychological insight
such as Horney's *Neurosis and Human Growth* as it is of books
dealing directly with the spiritual life. Assuming the material
is worthy, the manner of reading determines its usefulness for
prayer. We must read existentially. This means going beyond intellectual understanding and reacting personally and emotionally
to the work, using it as a mirror of oneself. Such existential
reading takes practice, for the parts we are most prone to reject
contain the material we most need, but, if the method is per-
fected, the divine Word will speak out of many a written page.
All this applies supremely to the Bible which is chiefly the record
of existential encounters between God and man. Scripture yields
its secrets only to the man who lets the words strike deep and
who is open to the changes which God may work in him.

Sometimes the operation of repentance and forgiveness needs
more than the facilitation of the spoken or written word. Ritual
and sacrament may serve to consummate the spiritual business
left unfinished. These may be simple rituals which a person
creates for himself, as when, for example, he writes his disturbing thoughts and commits them to the flames with a prayer of
thanksgiving that they are consumed by God's mercy. More

likely, however, these rituals will be the hallowed sacraments of the Church. Uncounted thousands have found that they receive the deepest sense of God's forgiveness while celebrating the Eucharist or Holy Communion with fellow Christians. Indeed, if the patterns suggested for confession are used in preparation for sacramental celebrations, unexpected power and reality will be released through them.

Another symbolic act which may be of use to those who find it hard to receive the mercy of God and who are haunted by guilt is symbolic penance. The ecclesiastical abuse of penance has long made it suspect for non-Roman Catholics. Nevertheless, we know that from earliest childhood something in us imposes penalties for guilt, evidently in order to establish some degree of psychological equilibrium. Among adults unconsciously self-imposed penalties often take the form of pain or illness which may eventuate in invalidism or death. The person literally condemns himself. If he could accept the love and forgiveness of God, he would be free of these consequences, but he finds such acceptance to be impossible. At such a juncture help may be found in symbolic penance. The sufferer names some penalty which he accepts in gratitude to God for His forgiveness. He must not think that he "buys" forgiveness, because this is both religiously and psychologically impossible, as Luther's penances so eloquently testify. Nevertheless, the unpleasant penance, supplying a concrete action to be performed, may become a means of lifting the person psychologically to a plane where he can fully accept God's mercy. Anyone who has worked with his own or another's guilt knows how creative the act of wholehearted acceptance of forgiveness may be.

There is admitted danger of obsessive introspection in these practices, but there is greater danger in neglecting them. Our safety lies in balancing confession with other kinds of prayer, and in balancing prayer with action. We must also conquer the

G

impatience that expects to accomplish the work of purgation in a day.

Impatience, which inclines a person to sporadic spurts and starts in religious discipline, must be conquered by a settled persistence. No rule of spiritual growth is more fundamental than the rule of persistence, the practice of coming back again and again despite failure, despite even the grossest and longest lapses. The despair or remorse which stand in the way of our persistence must be recognized as devices of the ego to protect itself. We have expended much labor and time building our ego shell, and a merciful God does not suddenly deprive us of it. Otherwise we should be terror-stricken to find ourselves standing ashamed and naked in the Presence òf the Real. We are as holy as we wish to be. The new births which we experience in spiritual development have each had a long gestation.

There is another reason for emphasizing persistence. Ego orientation is built into our social institutions and is reflected in our religious, political, and economic symbols of prestige and value. It takes time for us to recognize that these are illusions, and God cannot proceed with their destruction before the new Kingdom outlook is started. Otherwise we should be left helpless and distracted.

The confessional process is complicated by the difficulty of tracking down the devices through which the ego seeks to protect itself. These dodges must be exposed, but even after all the conscious part of us is willing, they sometimes are revealed only through years of experience.

A legend says that St. George, having slain the dragon, engaged in combat with the demon of falsehood and discovered that Christ himself protected the demon. Evil cannot be destroyed in a battle royal, because it will not die until all the truth which it conceals is made manifest. Then it will lose the very essence of its being and wither away.

Our impatience with the slowness of the process is a clue to
our pride. It annoys us that we are not already saints and that
there is much which still must be overcome. If only we were
in control of the processes of the universe, we would not have
to put up with delays and stupid interruptions! Our impatience
also reveals the absence in us of a vision of the good which God
is at this moment producing in His world. We are in effect chal-
lenging Him to do better. This is the old ego judging God Himself.

From his file of personal experiences, Leslie D. Weatherhead
illustrates the need for persistence. "A girl whom we will call
Mabel . . . was truly converted at one of the services in my old
church . . . she changed her way of looking at life and believed
the good news. . . . For a time she walked on air, but six weeks
after her conversion, she came into my vestry after an evening
service and said, 'I am giving up Christianity.' I was staggered
and said, 'Why?' She replied, 'Because it doesn't work. The
claims made for it are not substantiated. The goods promised
are not delivered.' These were not her exact words, but that was
the sense of her complaint. She told me quite candidly that she
had a bad temper which she had tried to master and help from
heaven had not been forthcoming. The sense of failure depressed
her beyond words.

"I cannot remember what I said to her. It is more than twenty
years ago. But I shall never forget what happened a minute or
two after she left the room. A man came into the room whom I
did not know, and he put down five pounds on my table as a
contribution to the Samaritan League. When I asked what had
prompted this generous gift, he said that his daughter had been
converted at one of our services and that the whole atmosphere
of his home had been altered. It did not take more than a second
or two for me to discover that it was Mabel's father, and he was
a little taken aback when I said, 'Go after her and fetch her

back.' He did not know that she had been in church that evening. They had not been sitting together. But you can imagine
the situation in that vestry when she came back into it with her
father."

We may learn wisdom from Christina Rossetti:

> Will the road wind uphill all the way?
> Yes, to the very end.
> Will the journey take the whole long day?
> From dawn to dusk, my friend.

On the importance of a slow, steady, and persistent pace,
Baron von Hügel retells the advice he received from a Dominican
priest, Father Hocking: "Had I noticed how mountaineers climb
mountains? How they have a quiet, regular, short step—on the
level it looks petty; but then this step they keep up, on and on
as they ascend, whilst the inexperienced townsman hurries along,
and soon has to stop dead-beat with the climb. That such an
expert mountaineer, when the thick mists come, halts and camps
out under some slight cover brought with him, quietly smoking
his pipe, and moving on only when the mist has cleared away."

Protestant thought and experience have often been too impressed by instantaneousness and suddenness in the religious life.
John Wesley was so anxious to deny any improvement or process
of growth through self-effort, that he assumed God's action in
both conversion and sanctification to be instantaneous. Though
there is an absolute qualitative difference between the ego and
the God-oriented life, the progress from one to the other, under
God's care, may be, and probably will be, slow.

Another device for deepening the moods of confession is the
practice of a moderate asceticism. The goal of prayer is the full
life through a spontaneous affirmation of existence in God's
world. On the way to this goal, however, some ascetic practices
may prove helpful. We may wisely reduce self-indulgence, com-

forts, and amusements, and seek small distasteful tasks that lie outside the sphere of duty. We may refuse to justify ourselves when criticized and willingly appear to be wrong even when we are right. We may pray to be unnoticed, anonymous, and without praise, thus avoiding all those temptations to self-glorification which arise in conversation, gossip, or storytelling.

We must remember that these practices are in themselves worthless. They could prove dangerous if we allow our pride to feed upon them. St. Paul, who painfully discovered for himself how dangerous such "works" could be, warns us in his letter to the fussy Colossians, "Don't let anyone worry you by criticising what you eat or drink, or what holy days you ought to observe, or bothering you over new moons or sabbaths. *All these things have at most only a symbolic value: the solid fact is Christ.* Nor let any man cheat you of your joy in Christ. [Do not] take the slightest notice of these purely human prohibitions—'Don't touch this,' 'Don't taste that' and 'Don't handle the other,' 'This,' 'that' and 'the other' will all pass away after use! I know that these regulations look wise with their self-inspired efforts at worship, their policy of self-humbling, and their studied neglect of the body. But in actual practice they do honour, not to God, but to man's own pride."

Jesus' experience with the righteous ascetics of his day and his joyful reception by those guilty of sensual faults led him to advise that all fasting should be done in secret and in such a way as to give no clue to others regarding the inner sacrifice. This effectively outmaneuvers the ego's wish for a holy reputation. But inward pride is the ego's countermove. We say to ourselves, I am the good person who sacrifices in secret! We must particularly rejoice in God during periods of discipline. Thus the surgery of mortification can perform its healing work without infection.

The young ruler turned sorrowfully away from Jesus "for he was very rich." The saints have rarely been wealthy or powerful, though there are important exceptions. Some camels do slip through the needle's eye, as Anatole France noted, "God's mercy is infinite: it will save even the rich."

The purpose of practicing simplification during the early phases of growth is to protect the tender spiritual impulses from the temptations of both possessions and authority. Later, when the soul has become strong in its purposes and knows the life within the Kingdom, then responsibilities of both property and position may be (perhaps must be) undertaken.

The corrupting effect of money and authority derives entirely from the ego. When the ego is dead and the soul is turned outward to all the good which God can bring to pass through our agency, we are then ready for any worldly calling.

In the materialistic climate of our culture it is easy to be deceived and unconsciously to equate the comfortable and the good life. Like John Woolman, who restricted his growing business so as to carry out his spiritual vocation, we must learn to control our possessions so that they do not control us.

There is a paradoxical relationship between this practice of simplicity and what has become known as the practice of abundance. We must learn, as St. Paul says, "how to be abased, and . . . how to abound." As sons of God, heirs of Him to whom everything in heaven and on earth belongs, abundance—a sufficiency for everything which needs doing in the Kingdom—should be a natural experience. Yet for brothers of Christ, who bore the Cross and allowed himself to be stripped of all things for our sakes, there is also a voluntary poverty which does not taste luxury while fellow human creatures lack necessities.

These aspects of the Kingdom are not contradictory; they complement one another. Out of our simplicity abundance comes, and because of our renunciation of all things, all things become ours. There is a time for abundance and a time for poverty. In Galilee, Jesus forbade his disciples to fast, told tales and performed deeds of abundance, ate and drank at wedding feasts, and led the disciples in a dance of joy; but in Jerusalem, during the last Passover, he led them into the shadow of nothingness and death.

Both experiences belong to those who are his brethren. Sometimes without guilt and with pure joy we experience the abundance of God. This often leads to an abundance to be shared by those who would have less if this joyfulness did not breed more abundance for all. At other times for his sake we willingly allow ourselves to be stripped of everything, and we bear the burden of our fellow sufferers.

These alternations are a matter of God's will for us. Only in a continuous humble offering of the whole of life to Him can we find for ourselves that perfect Will of the Eternal.

It is in order to find that perfect Will for our whole life, no area excluded, that we now turn to probing the chief areas in which we continue to resist Him.

CHAPTER 8

The Application

of Confession

Confession develops in two ways: through the spontaneous prayer described in the previous chapter, and through systematic confrontation with the demands of God. This second approach is required because, unfortunately, our popular concepts of sin do not cut across the real issues of life, and because most of the massive failures of Christians in so-called Christian civilization are not felt as proper material for confession. Both methods are important. They support each other. The way of spontaneous free expression of feeling clears the ground for the more demanding systematic analysis, and the systematic examination generates profounder feeling for spontaneous confession. By examining systematically the areas for confessional treatment we are progressively confronted by the larger dimensions of holiness and are carried far beyond conventional goodness into a life where God re-creates both man and culture.

All sin, "hidden" or open, is a fit subject for confessional prayer. In addition, conditions which, though not sinful in themselves, are favorable to sin need close examination. Typical examples include: inherited biological predispositions to anger, such as a nervous system easily triggered into defensive reactions; culturally inherited social conditions—institutions, ideas, programs—which are either defiant or neglectful of God; the accumulated effects of past sins; and childhood experiences in the family and neighborhood which may have built predispositions to act in egocentric ways. Though our lives are ruled by them, we may be largely unaware of these conditions and completely innocent of the knowledge that they have a strong bearing on our relationship to God. What follows is a systematic treatment of the major barriers to life in the Kingdom of God. It is offered to facilitate that difficult and searching work of self-exposure to the Light which both illuminates and heals. The first barrier is our old enemy egocentricity.

EGOCENTRICITY

The neurotic claim that "the universe should serve me" is the root of our resistance to God. Upon it rest the sins of pride and selfishness and all their monstrous offspring. The ego at the center of its own world is a tyrant that demands absolute allegiance and is capable of the most ingenious devices for securing it. When Reality continuously makes its tenure difficult and preposterous, the ego exerts more energy to resist the creative revolution of humility and love which would end its rule and establish the reign of heaven.

This evil can grow even in prayer and good works. Merely allow the ego to claim goodness as its own, and it will soon emerge with self-respect and social prestige. The Pharisees were very religious men who prayed, engaged in charitable acts, and supported every good work in the community, yet they were offended by the Reality which confronted them in Jesus Christ. Jesus saw that the same temptation would plague his own followers, so he warned them against assuming the righteous pose in judging others, the sin into which the righteous man most easily falls.

A remarkable exposure of the nature of egocentricity appears in Karen Horney's *Neurosis and Human Growth,* a wise harvest of years of psychoanalytic experience. The chief obstacle to authentic human growth, she writes, is the neurotic substitution of a pseudo-self for the real self, and the progressive organization of life and experience about that false center, which Shelley called the "dark idolatry of self." This ego begins a process of self-glorification and idealization which Miss Horney calls a "comprehensive neurotic solution," and the "energies driving toward self-realization [the deep authentic sources of growth] are shifted to the aim of actualizing the idealized self."

Self-glorification becomes the aim of the neurotic when the legitimate needs of personality growth are twisted into a whole system of "gigantic claims" against existence. "People whose need is to be always right feel entitled never to be criticized, doubted or questioned," Miss Horney writes in a passage of high significance for our understanding of egocentricity. "Those who are power-ridden feel entitled to blind obedience. Others, for whom life has become a game in which other people are to be skillfully manipulated, feel entitled to fool everybody and, on the other hand, never to be fooled themselves. Those who are afraid to face their conflicts feel entitled to 'get by,' to 'get around' their problems. The person who is aggressively exploiting, and intimidates others into letting him put something over on them, will resent it as unfair if they insist on a square deal. The arrogant, vindictive person, who is driven to offend others but yet needs their recognition, feels entitled to 'immunity.' Whatever he perpetrates on others, he is entitled to having nobody mind anything he does." Proceeding with this catalogue of neurotic claims operating in personal relations, she continues: "Another version of the same claim is the one for 'understanding.' No matter how morose or irritable one is, one is entitled to understand. The individual for whom 'love' is the over-all solution turns his need into a claim for exclusive and unconditional devotion. The detached person, seemingly quite undemanding, insists on one claim, however; not to be bothered. He feels that he does not want anything of others, and is therefore entitled to be left alone no matter what is at stake. 'Not to be bothered' usually implies being exempt from criticism, expectations, or efforts—even if these latter are on his own behalf."

These neurotic claims add up to the ego's attempt at self-glorification. But this glorification is, of course, contrary to the real self and its growth. It is primarily a devil's pact in which a life of false glory is exchanged for the authentic value found in the real person. It is Faust mirrored in each of us, or Jesus with the tempter in the wilderness, or Gautama with Mara under the Bo-tree; but we succumb, consent, yield. Even the painful consequences do not awaken us, because the damage of the present "is negligible in view of the prospect of the glorious future."

With its distorted self-evaluation, the ego develops a complete and tyrannous system of "shoulds." "The premise on which they operate is that 'nothing should be, or is, impossible for oneself.' The rule seems to be: 'Forget about the disgraceful creature you actually are; this is how you should be; and to be this idealized self is all that matters. You should be able to endure everything, to understand everything, to like everybody, to be always productive' to mention only a few of these inner dictates."

The solemnest warning is issued to those whose idealized image "lies in the direction of goodness, love and saintliness. They should be considerate, grateful, sympathetic, generous, loving, and so in their minds they have all these qualities." Despite all this "the neurotic does not gain what he most desperately needs: self-confidence and self-respect."

This neurotic pride in the ego image leads to deep self-hate, for the actual self which could grow and become something of worth is thought too base to be identified with oneself. Yet the real self is still alive and struggling to express its life. The result is a conflict between the ego and self, which Miss Horney calls the "central inner conflict." This conflict is almost unendurable, and the imagined self must exhaust all its energies to "protect himself from the disruptive power of the conflicts by finding pseudo solutions."

Miss Horney's work is a psychological description of the religious problem of sin in which man's heart, turned back upon itself, rejects God and His life for the false and damned life of defiance and separateness. The true self which Miss Horney recognizes as necessary to her system of analysis, I believe to be the "image of God," the potential Godward orientation of the finite creature, by which he participates in eternity and the unlimited life of God. I agree with Rufus Jones the Quaker mystic "that there is an unfathomable depth of inward Godlike being at man's spiritual centre which is the tap-root of human self-consciousness and which is unsundered from this Over-World which we call God." The problem of curing egocentricity is thus essentially a religious one. The true self which stands over against the ego as the high possibility of human personhood is located outside the range of psychological description. Again quoting Jones, this spiritual center is "deeper than our faculties, more fundamental than our ideas, or our images, or our volitions . . . , [it] is this subsoil root of our being, this essence of the soul, this core of personal personality, which is indissolubly connected with a higher world of reality and is the ground of mystical experience."

It is the religious dimension of egocentricity—or in traditional language, pride—which requires treatment through confessional prayer. Unwinding this encoiled life of the ego is impossible for the victim alone. Only God can unseat the pseudo-self, conquer pride, and resurrect the real self in spirit and in truth. Skilled counseling, either alone or in a group, when it is sympathetic to spiritual purposes, may hasten growth; but the ultimate reliance must be in God. He is the healing, whole-making power which underlies all therapy, and it is through prayer that we come directly into relation with Him. God's help, however, must not be confused with the pseudo-religious solutions—right "orthodoxies," revivalistic emotionalism, or "peace of mind" formulas —which alienate us from Him. Religious neuroses are, unfortunately, on the whole more resistant to healing than other pseudo-solutions to the human problem. Another pseudo-solution, likewise spawned by the self-encoiled ego, is anxiety.

ANXIETY

Anxiety is an inevitable by-product of self-sufficient pride. Building exaggerated claims against life and elaborating the "pride system" with its consequent self-hate and conflict, the ego is bound to regard every intrusion of Reality as a threat. As one of Miss Horney's patients complained, "Life is so terrible, it's so full of reality!" The ego life is thus pervaded by a basic anxiety which cannot be purged until the ego is dead. Before this death occurs, living is a constant strategy of escape and defense and always makes a person the victim of despair, more anxiety, and a host of compulsive—uncontrollable because unconsciously motivated—reactions.

A knowledge of the most *common forms of escape and defense* is a helpful background for the treatment of anxiety in confession. Pride and fear alike are often best recognized in their manifestations. Psychologists have not done much to illuminate the nature of true selfhood, but they have done massive research on these reality dodges, and a person bent on spiritual growth is wise to inform himself of their common forms:

Denial of the real self, or self-alienation through claiming that the ego is the real self, is a mechanism used by the ego to reduce its competition with the actual self.

Projection occurs when the ego attributes to others those basic drives in himself which he must deny in order to maintain his ego image. A person, for example, who tries to solve sex conflicts by repressing his own sex motives is apt to see sex intent in the most innocent behaviors of others.

Repression is necessary to self-esteem. The ego cannot believe itself to have the needs of ordinary persons and so denies the real forces in the personality. This denial may be so successful that no trace of the need remains in consciousness. A clue to the repressed needs appears when unusual feelings are experienced over trifles. We become angry or fearful at things which would not properly excite such emotions. If we pursue such feelings in prayer, their sources will be exposed.

Rationalization is a process of finding socially and personally acceptable reasons for acts, feelings, or opinions which would be rejected by others or by the ego. This leads to all sorts of deceptions and life is built around a huge involved lie. Training in sophisticated reasoning processes will only tend to make the lie more plausible.

Aggressive withdrawal into negativism—behaving perversely, as though one needed nothing from others, and rebuffing their approach, is a neurotic reaction. The pseudo-satisfaction which comes from the attention thus gained is substituted for the real satisfaction of needs. This is often observed in children whose rejective behavior is really motivated by an intense need for love. It has become common wisdom that the children who need love most are those who seem to deserve and desire it least.

Cynicism enables the ego to say: "All goodness is a pretense. The whole world is as bad or worse than I. Nothing matters anyhow. All idealism is pure romanticism." This, of course, excuses the pseudo-self from any of the claims of real value, and seems to establish the cynic as the supreme realist.

Psychic fragmentation, or compartmentalization, is a sealing off of certain systems of drives and ideas which allows them to function in isolation from conflicting systems. In extreme cases this may result in multiple personality. However, even in the normal ranges of behavior we all employ this device to some extent. The only possibility of genuine integration is on the basis of Reality-orientation, and this is costly. To the ego it means death.

Fantasy, or daydreaming, is an imaginative fulfillment of desires. It is an escape from the difficulties of real life into a realm where all obstacles to success can be ignored or effectively surmounted. Escape fiction and drama often serve as pseudo-fulfillments and become substitutes for genuine actualizations in the real world.

Regression is a retreat to simpler forms of behavior and satisfactions which were enjoyed at earlier stages of growth. A companion difficulty is fixation, getting stuck at certain levels of growth and refusing to mature beyond them.

Rigidity is the attempt to crystallize life into unassailable structure of fixed beliefs, patterns of activity, and attitudes. Craving for certainty leads to the "true believer," the man who must have absolute answers to every question. He is unable to endure the flexibility and uncertainty which true growth demands. If he is religious, he demands detailed promises and creeds which leave no room for the unexpected or unanswered. In political and economic matters he exhibits the same characteristics. The old rigid structures have to be melted down, genuine doubts have to be admitted, and the tensions of true inquiry and growth have to be endured. This is one possible meaning of Jesus' advice to Nicodemus, you have to be born again, return to the flexibility and humility of the growth process.

These devices of escape and defense have well-defined psychic consequences. They increase anxiety, despite the fact that they were employed to decrease it. In addition, the personality is flooded with unhappiness, despair, and self-pity. Behavior, furthermore, deteriorates into mechanicalness, phobias, and com-

pulsions; and aversions to foods, animals, ideas, situations, or
people become obsessive.

Dealing with anxiety in confession: Recalling the first pattern
of confession, let the mind and imagination play freely on the
above topics which seem most relevant to our own need. The
basic questions are: Am I afraid of persons, situations, possible
events? What defenses and escapes am I employing to reduce my
feeling of fear without dealing with the real situations and relationships of life?

Then, reflect that in the light of God's sovereign power and
love we can, if necessary, accept the worst in these negative
situations. This reflection aims at an inner invulnerability which
is not neurotic detachment, but a realization of the dynamic
security of a life "hid with Christ in God." The test of the
authenticity of this inner peace comes when we face the very
things we have feared and discover that we have a dynamic and
creative freedom to accept and deal with them.

From this posture of invulnerability it is possible to deal with
the aspects of the situation which are capable of solution. This
involves first scouting all the relevant facts in the fear situation
and looking at them squarely. The next step is to analyze the
meaning of these facts: Why are they a problem? What patterns
do they exhibit? Then analysis must lead to decision upon a
course of action, a decision not based upon certainties, but upon
a willingness to accept risks which flout the ego's need for
security. Finally, comes the action itself.

To each stage of this problem-solving work prayer brings its
powerful if invisible support. Through prayer God gives man the
courage to face reality, illuminates the meaning of the situations
which threaten, steadies his wavering will to act, and even reorders the events into which his actions must fit. God is active at
every level of the difficulties which perplex us. "In everything,"
testifies St. Paul, "God works for good with those who love him."

HATE

Anger, bitterness, resentment, and hatred of self and others spring, as does fear, from ego orientation and pride. Fear begets hate, for it leads us to perceive all reality as a threat. Hot anger is a device for reducing personal tensions which arise in the presence of problems, but it does not direct attention to the objective problematic situation. Rather it is half-blinded by the smoke of its own emotions. Jesus, more than any other religious teacher, described the spiritual peril of anger and contempt, even when that bitterness was directed toward "enemies." To become angry is to be overcome by evil; whereas Jesus taught that we are to "overcome evil with good."

Of course we will justify ourselves. Our anger is always "righteous indignation" directed at crimes against the weak or innocent. We immediately think of the times when Jesus cleansed the Temple or denounced the Pharisees, and we justify ourselves accordingly. The flaw in our rationalization lies in our use of the word "anger" to include both the ego-less emotion of the saint and the petulant irritation of the proud. No doubt something that looks very much like our "anger" appears from time to time in the lives of highly developed spiritual men, but there is a difference. What that difference is cannot be known directly to us until our emotional life ceases to be tied to the destiny of the ego and its pride system. Until then it is sound spiritual advice to forego anger and use the pent-up feelings to carry us forward swiftly in confession to God.

The ultimate purpose is to discover the desire to love and be loved that lies behind all our hatred and fanatical rejection. Behind hate is a fear of being depreciated, counted as nothing, or being rejected, and behind fear is also the longing to give and receive deeply. This is our real Self which is the energy behind even the ego. This humbling need for love emerges powerfully

H

in the permissive presence of God. It grows into a passion to express toward all beings, freely and without guilt, the current that flows from the divine center. This is no saint or martyr complex, but rather a reflection of Reality and our ultimate orientation toward it.

GUILT

Proper guilt must be distinguished from pseudo-guilt. Proper guilt is a feeling of shame in the face of Reality, in the presence of God. Surrounded by such holiness, all the imperfections of the inner life are revealed, just as ringworm fungus glows in ultraviolet light. Pseudo-guilt shares the same feeling, but it is the ego's reaction to its own pride system, to its own impossible system of "shoulds" and "should-nots," to its own rage at not being perfect. It is a form of self-punishment which balances the economy of the inner life. Only an acceptance of the actual self and a contentment with its real possibilities for growth can banish pseudo-guilt. Real guilt disappears when the mercy of God is clearly seen and accepted through humble prayer.

The humility to see oneself as a real sinner is an act of grace: to recognize that the habitual rejection of love and creativity has incurred an unlimited liability; to sense the wasted and irrecoverable past, the unproductive present, and the mortgaged future. But grace, which unveils sin in order to remove it, gives also the vision of mankind as it came to Mother Juliana, "all-mannerful enclosed in the mildness of God." Within that loving enclosure the need for self-punishment by guilt and its accompaniments—loneliness, sickness, and fear—dies away, and forgiveness becomes real. This forgiveness is not a static state of sinlessness. Man never comes to the place where he may dispense with grace. Human life is a reciprocating experience of repentance and restoration leading to endless growth in creativity and love.

Even here the ego has a last dodge, the formula "I am too

great a sinner to be forgiven by God." Real acceptance of forgiveness requires the ego to die by denying itself even this last
vanity of being chief of sinners. Many Christians who formally
believe in forgiveness and even pray for it continue to retain
feelings of guilt and do not realize that this is a secret distrust
and even defiance of God.

The method for dealing with guilt is similar to the methods
for handling anxiety or hatred. It is important to master the
skill of following feelings and completely accepting them.
Nothing is too trifling, if it makes us feel ill at ease and guilty.
If it should turn out to be pseudo-guilt, then it can be recognized
as such. When we discover that many of our "shoulds" and
"should-nots" are neurotic projections of our false role as a
"perfect self," we will find them dropping away. Some of this
pseudo-guilt is a reaction to the conflict of conventional morals,
the contradictory nature of the behavior and attitudes expected
of us as members of society. For example, an American woman
will find herself expected to be a Hollywood beauty, a perfect
cook and housekeeper, a model mother for her children, a
glamorous wife, an intelligent and athletic companion for her
husband, and an unfailing worker in all civic and religious
groups. She will inevitably fail and feel guilty unless she recognizes the purely conventional nature of these "expectations" and
"roles" which are imposed upon her by society. Then she will
be free to let her real self and her authentic vocation before
God become the standard of her work. The pseudo-guilts will
melt away.

Some of our guilts are deeply rooted in the way we were
treated as children. Even in adulthood we continue to be little
children who try to please a tyrannous parent and hope that by
compliance we may restore the primitive harmony of mother-
father-brother-sister. If someone frowns, we ask, What have I
done? When a friend expresses anger or annoyance, we become

conscience-smitten and search for the fault which caused the breach.

Or we may try to fulfill the impossible roles which our frustrated parents, compensating for their own failures, imposed upon us. So we blame ourselves for failing in what was impossible at the outset. The only remedy is to pray through these primal relationships with our parents, brothers, and sisters—all the primary group—until as a real person we stand in a genuine relationship with each of them. Naturally, since these encounters have taken place over long periods of time and during the most formative parts of our life, the healing process will be slow and painful. But it is necessary and supremely rewarding.

These things must not only be recognized intellectually; they must be felt and inwardly accepted. Prayer is the most creative environment for this insight and the only mood in which genuine forgiveness can be coupled with the dispelling of pseudo-guilt.

Let us recall the suggested procedure outlined before: Surrender all sins, real and imaginary, to God who already knows them. Accept His forgiveness and complete and unbounded release from them. Express trust in His forgiveness by thanking Him. Finally, put the experience of forgiveness to the test by living affirmatively in both thought and action.

INFERIORITY

Pride would seem to be the invulnerable armor against inferiority, but it is only an iron maiden whose spikes pierce to the heart and brain. Pride generates inferiority by its system of impossible standards, its perfectionism, its refusal to admit a flaw of any kind. The actual self is a much poorer thing than the shining ego image, but only by the acceptance of that self and its growth can inferiority be ended.

Willingness to be the unique person we are in God's sight is the only cure for inferiority. This is made difficult, however, by our life experiences. All of us at one time or another have been deprived of a perfect response to our own needs, physical or spiritual, and the rest of our lives may reflect that deficiency. We may, like the neurotic, crave love to an insatiable degree and so make gigantic claims against others in order to guarantee our own safety or comfort. The psychologist A. H. Maslow believes this to be so fundamental in our make-up that he classifies human beings into two groups: *Those who are growth motivated and those who are deficiency motivated.* Deficiency-motivated people are incapable of receiving satisfaction from life or love. They can not satisfy the genuine needs of growth, because a deficiency in their past has grown into a monstrous chasm which cannot be filled. Such people do not behave as though they felt inferior; they exhibit an offensive superiority that demands all and gives nothing. Yet at heart they are empty and poor, and they are doomed to remain so until they experience *metanoia,* a change of heart and mind which sets their faces toward Reality rather than toward the ego.

C. S. Lewis delineates another form which inferiority takes. In the novel *That Hideous Strength* he portrays a man who is tempted by his weakness to be "in" with a select "inner ring" and the process by which he is led gradually from the relatively innocent satisfaction of his ego deficiency to the verge of monstrous crime. The "Inner Ring" as he describes it in an earlier essay, is that coveted select group, reception to whose company the ego believes to be the gateway to a heaven of all satisfactions. But once inside he discovers that these people are just like those on the outside, and that there is yet beyond another coveted "inner ring." This "inner ring" complex gives select groups their social power. The mature, released, self-actualizing person is not tempted. He knows that his happiness will depend upon the fulfillment of the authentic creative work of his life and not upon admission to any inner group, however select.

POWER

Power, though not an adequate satisfaction for the inner needs of the self, is another temptation for the inferior soul. Unfortunately, it is not limited by physical structures as are gluttony or sexual lust. The domination of others gives the ego a keen satisfaction which must grow to feed the insatiable craving. The ego-power drive has as its objective more power and yet more power. Furthermore, it must reduce to slaves and puppets those whom it dominates, making them devoid of any center of decision of their own. As long as anyone retains some self-actualizing freedom, the ego is insecure and must still find means to prove its superiority. This lure of mastery, as Miss Horney calls it, is clearly another pseudo-solution in the conflict raised in the depths of personality by our identification with a false self.

ADDICTION

The tensions and unhappiness of the ego life inevitably drive us toward the habitual use of detentioners. *Lust* and *gluttony* are two common forms of degeneration. "Erotic love lures this type [the ego-oriented]," writes Miss Horney, "as the supreme fulfillment. Love must and does appear as the ticket to paradise, where all woe ends: no more loneliness; no more feeling lost, guilty, and unworthy; no more responsibility for self; no more struggle with a harsh world for which he feels hopelessly un-equipped. Instead love seems to promise protection, support, affection, encouragement, sympathy, understanding."

But the ego is really incapable of love. Every relationship will degenerate into lust, wherein the other person is used merely as a means to the satisfaction of the pseudo-self. Although sex is necessarily greatly overvalued in an ego-oriented society like our own, our individual sexual adjustment is an essential clue to the degree of our own maturity. The neurotic cannot be sexually

adjusted, but, because of the intense way in which sexual experience involves his whole being, he may become aware of his
neurosis precisely at this point. The promise and the disappointment are equally great, and in the face of such deep frustrations
the actual self may have its chance to break the tyranny of the
ego.

Gluttony is another potential ticket to paradise, but it has
this advantage over erotic love, there is no other person with
whom to bother. Pleasure, to ease the anxieties of the ego life,
may be had by a continuous stimulation of the oral cavity. By
aptly reducing the inner tensions perpetually generated in the
conflict of ego with Reality, eating, drinking, smoking, and all
the rich possibilities of sensual enjoyment may postpone in-
definitely our having to deal with the basic conflicts of life.

GREED

Greed and avarice have no realistic objective. Their purpose
is to reassure the precariously situated ego by piling about it the
illusions of physical security and the distractions of innumerable
toys. There is also the lure of respectability which our society
ascribes to the wealthy even though all other admirable qualities
may be missing. Greed is a temptation not merely to those who
have the real possibility of great wealth, but even to those who
remain poor. No symptom of spiritual poverty is more revealing
than the pettiness of our clutching for possessions. We are
ashamed to have little and to appear poor, because our spiritual
treasures are so meager. The spiritually mature men are those
who often have chosen poverty or have willingly refused to
escape from it. "Foxes have holes, and birds of the air have nests,
but the Son of man has nowhere to lay his head." There is, of
course, the pride of poverty which in its way is as revealing of
spiritual emptiness as pride of possessions. Alexander of Macedon
is said to have remarked to Diogenes who was sitting in rags
outside the city of Athens, "I can see your pride through the

holes in your garments." By contrast, the young Gautama, by leaving behind a kingdom with all its power and riches, disencumbered himself for the spiritual quest.

Our world is acutely aware of the spiritual issue of possessions. No one who indulges in luxuries while nine-tenths of humanity suffers from the lack of necessities can speak to the problems of our century. No wonder that the most powerful voice in Asia has been that of Gandhi, wedded like St. Francis to poverty.

DRIFT

Biologists recognize two tendencies in living organisms: anabolic, the tendency to grow and build up the organism, and catabolic, the tendency to decay, grow old, decline. In physics this latter is called "entropy," which means that all physical systems "run down" unless they are replenished by fresh energy from the outside. Both of these tendencies work in man's body. In addition, there appears to be a spiritual entropy, which is a principle of drift.

In his reconstruction of logic, John Dewey begins with the assumption that man will not think unless jogged into awareness by a problem. When the problem passes, he naturally returns to a state of passive contentment. In the arena of history, Arnold Toynbee contends that civilizations arise because of great "challenges" to which men have given a creative "response." But he warns that such a response is not automatic and that the descendants of this same "creative minority" may choose to "rest on their oars," become a mere "dominant minority," and finally drift to cultural death.

Gerald Heard's survey of biological evolution leads to similar conclusions. There is a tendency for species to meet the environmental problem with the obvious and easy solution. Large claws or teeth make easy the killing of prey. Sheer bulk, hoofs, or wings give protection from enemies. The whole world of subhuman creatures seems to be a museum of odd specialties highly "adapted" to specific environmental situations. But these adaptations, like the rigid adaptation of certain civilizations and personalities, are often an entombment. There is no way back to the more demanding and exhilarating generalized structures which, though not adapted to any specific environment, are capable of solving an infinite range of yet unforeseen problems.

The "entropic" running-down process seems, then, to be all-pervasive and is exhibited in biology, physics, history, and personality. Cromwell recognized this principle in the spiritual life when he wrote in the fly leaf of his Bible: "He that is not getting better is getting worse."

The spiritual life is dynamic. We are not yet what we are to be, or as St. John said, "It does not appear what we shall be." The British philosopher T. H. Green has said that the nature of man is "in process of being communicated to him," for he is not yet a species. This growth requires the most strenuous effort. Anything which shocks us awake and forces us to exert ourselves should be welcomed as a gift of grace.

Martin Buber recounts a tale of the later Hasidim: "When Rabbi Yaakov Yitzhak was young and had board and lodging in the house of his father-in-law, his next door neighbor was a smith. The smith got up very early in the morning and struck hammer on anvil until the sound roared like thunder in the ears of the sleeping youth. Yaakov Yitzhak woke up and thought: 'If this man tears himself away from sleep so early for worldly work and worldly profit, shall I not be able to do the same for the service of the eternal God?' The following morning he rose before the smith, who, as he entered his smithy, heard the young man reading in a low tone. This irritated him: 'There he is at work already, and he doesn't need to! I certainly won't let a fellow like that get ahead of me!' On the following night he got up before the Yehudi. But the young rabbi took up the challenge and won the race. In later years he used to say: 'Whatever I have attained I owe first and foremost to a smith.' "

IDOLATRY AND DOUBLE-MINDEDNESS

In the book of Second Kings it is written that King Ahaz of Jerusalem, going to Damascus to meet Tiglathpileser, the king of Assyria, saw the altar that was in that place. He was so impressed that he sent the specifications of it to his high priest in Jerusalem with instructions that a replica be built and installed in the Temple. "And the bronze altar which was before the Lord he removed from the front of the house, . . . and put it on the north side of the altar."

This is a model of the two altars in our inner spiritual court wherein the altar of the Lord is set off to one side. Ahaz still had a superstitious awe concerning it and specified that at times "the bronze altar shall be for me to inquire by." This double-mindedness is a grotesque spiritual tragedy. Elijah speaks to our condition when he demands, "How long will you hobble on this faith and that?" And the Lord says, "If therefore thine eye be single, thy whole body shall be full of light. But if thine eye be evil [double], thy whole body shall be full of darkness. If therefore the light that is in thee be darkness, how great is that darkness!"

There are many modern forms of idolatry, such as abstract intelligence worshiped as the whole truth; special deified groups like the nation, race, or class; or humanity elevated to the place of God. There is the worship of the Past, the illusion of archaism; the Present, the illusion of final truth in the *status quo;* and the Future, the illusion of Utopia. All of these idolaters the historian Toynbee has exposed.

These idols are God-eclipsing because they do not fall within any of the popular so-called "immoralities." They are worse than sensuality because, appearing as angels of light, in reality they are demons of darkness. Worship of these "gods" has justi-

fied and promoted nearly every demonic evil current in our day.
Even humanism, which seems so good because it includes all
men, is not God. As the prophet writes:

> Cursed is the man who trusts in man,
> And makes flesh his arm of strength,
> His mind being turned from the Lord!
> He shall be like a scrub in the desert,
> Unable to see the coming of good;
> He shall dwell in the scorched lands of the wilderness,
> In an uninhabited salt land.

> Blessed is the man who trusts in the Lord,
> To whom the Lord is his confidence!
> He shall be like a tree planted by waters,
> That sends out its roots to the stream;
> And is not afraid when heat comes,
> For its leaves remain green
> Nor is anxious in a year of drought,
> For it ceases not to bear fruit.

Our own private idolatry often takes the form of some special
area of life which we specify as our own and from which we
exclude God. Only when all this, as well as our larger idols, is
utterly surrendered can the power of God flow through us in
transforming prayer.

Ignorance has not always been regarded as a spiritual vice. On
the contrary, learning and reason have been pointed out as
enemies of simple piety. Scientific investigation has been suspected of presumptuous curiosity seeking to overpass the limits
set for man. Man's primal sin, according to the legend of Eden,
consisted of eating from the tree of knowledge against the express prohibition of God himself. Despite this, the plain fact is
that ignorance is a curse which leads to the most tragic personal
and social consequences. Spiritual living requires hard thinking.

The "thoughtlessness" of modern man has been noted by

Albert Schweitzer who feels a special calling to promote ele-
mental thinking. It is growingly apparent that only if men aim
at a life of vigorous thought, understood as a spiritual achievement, turning aside from the hypnotic sleep of ready-made and
conventional notions, can they share in creative solutions to the
manifold perplexities of modern global civilization.

When the factors which distort the human perception of
reality are recognized, it is clear that the defeat of ignorance
may be rightly called a spiritual achievement. The nervous system, first of all, is primarily geared to action and reaction, not
to reflection. A stimulus leads directly to a response, unless it
is inhibited by some strong force. This was quite satisfactory when
man lived in relatively primitive conditions in a simple environment. In complex civilized life, however, man has to retrain the
basic set of the body to different responses. He has to learn to
inhibit action and stimulate thought—to "stop and think." He
must cultivate the habit of examining the forces which stimulate
him and evaluate their consequences. Only then is he prepared
to react wisely to what confronts him. As long as he fails in this
he is the easy victim of those who seek to manipulate him for
their own purpose. He finds himself responding automatically to
to such stimuli as slogan words, the color of a man's skin, the
accent of his speech, or the emotional outcries of the latest
editorial. He does not intend evil, but he does it just the same.

The human nervous system and its primitive reactions are
not the only problem in the conquest of ignorance. One's personal history also conditions him to see the world in a set way.
He projects upon the world the feelings and attitudes which
have their origin in events long past. He takes for sober truth
those judgments which merely reflect the state of the digestive
system or a long forgotten encounter with his father.

Culture, too, may be added to the forces which distort human
judgment. Class, nationality, race, religious heritage, and the

specific memberships and social roles for which men are responsible, all function to complicate the process of accurately assessing the world.

Although there is no "angelic" mentality available to man which relieves him of these liabilities to ignorance—he must continually struggle with them—confessional prayer is one place where the strictly human biases may be recognized for what they are. Here the pride which grows so inveterately within our systems of knowledge may be continuously challenged without one's falling into the despair of complete skepticism. Furthermore, when men pray for vision and submit to the labors of patient inquiry, truth does break out of the circle of these inauspicious conditions.

Unfortunately, the average devout Christian is completely unaware that these factors are operating in such a way as to distort his view of God's world. He imagines himself to share God's perspective on events and values when in truth he is almost entirely conventional in his appraisals. His judgments are the same as those made by the average non-Christian of his own class and culture. He has no inspired "prophetic" evaluation of the social forces which rapidly are shaping the future for good or ill. He ignorantly co-operates with them. He has only to compare himself to a prophet such as Isaiah to realize that God does not will us to remain ignorant servitors of accustomed evil. Through prayer and meditation, informed by intelligent study and reflection, there will gradually dawn some glimpses of events seen in the perspective of eternity.

There is no end to this process. We should be aware of the pretentiousness of imagining that there is a "once-for-all" liberation from distorted judgments. There is no human infallibility.

Ignorance is perpetuated by the pretense to "knowledge" which is embodied in rigid theologies, "scientific" systems, and dogmatic ideologies. Confronted by ambiguity in events it is natural that we should crave some answer, some meaning. But this craving for meaning can lead us to clutch frantically at premature solutions which in turn become "final truth" for us. Kierkegaard says that we must learn to live over seventy thousand fathoms of water. There is no way of coming to shore and finding the hard earth of surety beneath our feet. Reality will buoy us up and respond to our faith, if we trust ourselves to it and stop seeking fixed finality. The only genuine finality for us is to live constantly in interaction with the mysterious living God who is within and about us, and to trust the holy Spirit which forever leads us into all truth.

CONFESSION CONCLUDED: THE GREAT METHOD

The two main approaches to confession—the free confessional method of the preceding chapter, and the systematic method of the present one—must be placed in the larger setting of the sanctifying work which God performs in us every moment of our life. The total acceptance of His unremitting work in us I call the great method in confession. This method, as J. P. de Caussade has said in his devotional classic, *Abandonment to Divine Providence*, "consists in willing what comes to us by the order of God." This means to look upon the whole range of our experience as food for spiritual growth. Fritz Kunkel waves the stump of his left arm and smilingly says, "I was psychoanalyzed by the first world war." Unfortunately, to learn from experience requires that we find in it a sense of purpose and meaning, however painful. It means to "will it" to happen as it happens and to "accept it" as it happens in the way it happens. De Caussade writes, "Whatever value in itself of meditation, contemplation, vocal prayer, interior silence, acts of the will whether sensible, distinct, or less perceptible, retreat, or active life— *better than all of them is what God wills for the soul at the present moment;* and the soul should regard everything else with perfect indifference, as being of no value whatever."

The modern reader may be offended by this doctrine. It sounds like fatalism, predestination, or worse, to say that God wills evil and pain for his creatures. It is none of these. The criticism is beside the point. This doctrine is not speculative on these matters. It is primarily an advice concerning our inner attitude toward the onging of events. We are advised to use all experience as a teacher, and to humble ourselves to pain, success, suffering, or joy, and to extract substance for spiritual growth from each. We may leave aside questions of theodicy—how God's power and the evil in existence may be reconciled. This method merely says that we must not imagine that the food for spiritual growth lies elsewhere than where we now stand. God makes it possible for every event, whatever its cause, to assist us toward maturity. This lies at the base of de Caussade's concept of "abandonment or absolute surrender to divine providence." "The soul that is not united solely to the will of God will find neither rest nor sanctification in any self-chosen means—not even in the most excellent exercises of piety," he writes. "If that which God himself chooses for you does not suffice, what other hand can minister to your desires? If you turn from the food the divine will itself has prepared for you, what viands will not prove insipid to a taste so depraved? A soul cannot be truly nourished, strengthened, purified, enriched, sanctified, except by the fullness of the present moment."

Our self-chosen means of sanctification often miss the point and merely enhance our pride. The ego cunningly directs us to those austerities and disciplines which we least need, but which show up best. The ongoing course of life's events pays no such heed to the ego's demands and wishes. Acceptance of these is truly the training in humility and trust which we need. "God reveals himself to us as mysteriously, as adorable and with as much reality in most ordinary events as in the great events of history and the holy scriptures." Of course, both the Book and experience are equally enigmatic except to the eye of faith.

To the man who can trust in God's providence, however, "the revelation of the present moment is an inexhaustible source of sanctity." "It is no longer either prayer or silence, retirement or conversation, reading or writing, reflections or cessation of thought, avoidance or seeking of spiritualities, abundance or privation, illness or health, life or death, but simply what comes to her [the soul] each moment by the order of God."

This life of self-abandonment to divine providence releases all that sense of self-importance, spiritual busyness, yes, even religious greediness, which forever keep us on the margins of the Kingdom. Some years ago Allan Hunter, speaking about a friend who was dying of cancer of the throat, said, "He has just enough time to become a saint." Unfortunately, Bishop Fénelon is right when he says, "We suffer, but we don't allow the mission of suffering to be accomplished in us." The mission of suffering is to reveal our self-centeredness, our true loves, our dependence upon comfort and outward things.

Suffering is a great mystery, and we do not wish to suggest a cheap answer. We know, however, that it has great uses for spiritual maturation. The words of de Caussade again point the way: "Who can cope with the Almighty, whose ways are inscrutable?" "A life of self-abandonment is characterized by mystery; it is a life which receives from God extraordinary miraculous gifts through commonplace fortuitous events, chance encounters, where nothing is visible to human eyes but the ordinary workings of men's minds and the natural course of the elements."

When this self-abandonment to God has become habitual and the eye of faith has turned from preoccupation with inner spiritual problems and opened onto the commonplace circumstances of life, confession merges quite naturally into the prayer of petition.

CHAPTER 9

Petition

and God's Creativity

Petition is the trustful offering of clarified human need and longing to the overarching fatherliness of God in prayer. "Its basis lies," as Andrew Murray wrote years ago, "in God's entire willingness to grant, and our right as sons to claim." Jesus said, "Whatever you ask in prayer, you will receive, if you have faith."

At the Roman Catholic shrine at Lourdes, France, Charles McDonald of Dublin was healed in September, 1936, of what his physicians regarded as a hopeless illness. An abstract of his case history was taken one year later by Dr. Smiley Blanton of New York from the *Bureau des Constatationes Medicale* of Lourdes, at which time Dr. Blanton was able personally to examine the patient. The following summary of the facts of the case are taken from this abstract which was reported in 1939 to a joint meeting of the American Psychoanalytic and American Psychiatric Associations.

When McDonald arrived at Lourdes on Saturday, September

5, 1936, he was suffering intense pain from tuberculosis of the lungs, a tubercular infection of the spine which had destroyed the twelfth thoracic vertebra, and a similar infection of the shoulder which had practically destroyed the bony structure of the joint. Pockets of similar infection were exuding pus from both sides of his back, and urine specimens revealed albumin, blood cells, and granular and hyaline casts, highly suggestive that the infection had also reached the kidneys. For fifteen months he had been unable to leave his bed, and doctors in Dublin had declared him a hopeless case.

The patient was bathed at the Shrine on Sunday morning, September 6, and again on the next day, after which he began to feel a "glow of health." Within a few hours he was convinced that he had experienced a miraculous healing. With his highest expectations fulfilled, he left for home on Wednesday night, September 9.

In accordance with the rules of Lourdes for declaring an official healing, McDonald returned to the Shrine a year later and was examined by the medical bureau and also by Dr. Blanton. He bore with him the written testimony of a Dublin physician dated August 27, 1937, which read: "I have seen Mr. McDonald twice since his return from Lourdes. I can definitely say that there is no appearance of any former maladies. Mr. McDonald is a clean, active man who can accomplish his work without fatigue and without misery. All his old wounds were perfectly healed." A further X-ray examination in the Medical Bureau at Lourdes revealed the marks of the tubercular infections on bones of the back and shoulder and on the lungs and kidneys, but no sign of active disease. The scars were there, but the infection was gone.

Dr. Blanton insists that the healing was genuine, that all records were adequate and made by well-trained and reputable physicians. "Furthermore," he points out, "this is not an isolated case but one of approximately ten or twelve that occur at Lourdes yearly in which the records seem well and honestly made."

Here we have an instance of the creative work of God proceeding in an atmosphere of religious faith and prayer. What seems to have occurred is a remarkable speeding up of the recuperative and healing processes of the body. Vital processes were somehow enhanced, and the drift of the organism toward death was halted. In states of prayer this remarkable release of creative power is a common occurrence: bodies are knit up, minds and spirits are made whole, and social relationships are reconciled.

The background of this creativity is the sovereign, loving, and holy Creator whom men discover in adoration and confession. If adoration is the celebration of that awesome Reality, petition is a form of participation with Him in loving creativity. He shares His mysterious powers with us by joining our deepest desires and longings to Him in prayer.

We have seen in the example of healing something of the creative Power in whose hands we are and to whom our prayers are entrusted. Let us turn to a broader examination of the dimensions of God's creativity which is at work in many diverse ways throughout the universe.

The Bible begins with the miracle of creation: "In the beginning God created the heavens and the earth. . . ." But many Christians do not realize that He continues to create, and that without His ceaseless activity all would resolve into chaos and nothingness. The Apostle Paul saw in Christ and the experience of the early Church, the continued creation of God who "in everything works for good with those who love him." In this he echoed the words of Jesus, "My Father is working still, and I am working."

We see the world as a stable, mechanical order and often fail to perceive the incessant torrent of forces which keeps that order in existence. Like the image on a television screen which appears to be firm and rigid, yet is sustained by a bombardment of billions of electromagnetic impulses, so the macroscopic order of physical events is the average of inconceivable totals of atomic and molecular events too minute for our senses to grasp. What appears stable and too dense and rigid to dissolve is now known by science to be whirling packets of enormous activity. In so describing physical reality, twentieth-century scientists have made it possible to appreciate the continuing activity of the Creator in nature.

Professor Hoyle's theory of continuous material creation has been referred to in Chapter 5. He and his colleagues describe how throughout interstellar space freshly created particles of matter cluster first into gaseous thin clouds and then swirl into ever denser forms, finally bursting into flaming suns whose energy is nourished by the transmutation of matter itself. These swirling celestial fires are not merely single stars, but systems of stars within systems of stars. Hundreds of millions of them move in the rhythm which produces the galaxies. Furthermore, each galaxy, vast though it is, is merely one of uncounted millions of others which are separated by spaces that take light a billion years to traverse. This is the universe which God sustains by "the right hand of His power."

Within the more visible portions of the world the creative work also continues. Millions of snowflakes fall each day upon the earth. Each one is a perfect crystal that obeys the laws of Euclid's geometry. Yet in this pageant of order and novelty no two are ever alike. Physical science has in the past been so intent upon similarities in nature that individual differences and changes over long periods were not noticed. But modern science now describes the laws of nature as the temporary habits of a vast organism which is changing and moving at every level from the galaxies to the atom.

The creative work of God can be seen even more easily in the biological world. New organisms, each different from its parents and from all its contemporaries or descendants, grow from seeds to maturity. The divine work appears in the healing of a wound wherein new flesh repairs the wholeness (holiness) of the body. Among the mentally ill the pressure toward wholeness and individuality is the chief reliance of the psychotherapist. He helps the patient release the inherent forces of health and integration within his own being.

Personality at its highest is a work of the greatest creation, combining, as a work of art, a maximum of variety and richness with the maximum of integrity and wholeness. The same creative pattern can be traced in the social process by which small isolated tribes are gradually collected first into city states, then into countries, and today are growing toward some form of universal society.

In nature and history the creative process is seen from the outside, but in artistic creation, scientific discovery, or moral and spiritual growth the mystery of creation is encountered directly within.

"What were virtue, love, patriotism, friendship," writes Shelley in his *Defense of Poetry*, "what were the scenery of this beautiful universe which we inhabit; what were our consolations this side of the grave—and what were our aspirations beyond it, if poetry did not ascend to bring light and fire from those eternal regions where the owl-winged faculty of calculation dare not ever soar? Poetry is not like reasoning, a power to be exerted according to the determination of the will. A man cannot say, 'I will compose poetry.' The greatest poet cannot even say it; for the mind in creation is as a fading coal, which some invisible influence like an inconstant wind, awakens to transitory brightness; this power arises from within, like the color of a flower which fades and changes as it develops, and the conscious portions of our nature are unprophetic either of its approach or its departure. Could this influence be durable in its original purity and force, it is impossible to predict the greatness of the results."

How similar to these words is Jesus' comment to Nicodemus about the Spirit which comes like the wind and "we know not whence it cometh or whither it goeth." It is not a great leap of thought to think of Jesus' continuous re-creative work as simply the continuance of this "influence" in its "original purity and force," and with what results: the healing of the sick, the restoration of the sinner, the dissolving of guilt, the unleashing of divine love, the rechanneling of history; in short, the unfolding of the Kingdom of God. This is the secret of Jesus' overwhelmingly redemptive work. Life after life he brought into the holy center of the Kingdom where health, moral vigor, and spiritual vitality were restored. In his presence every alien element was transformed, as clay in the potter's hands, into fresh beauty and meaning. The Cross is the supreme instance of this transformation. Here the pain and shame of an execution assume significant form as a revelation of the divine compassion and holiness of Eternity.

With his usual gift of insight Goethe traced the relationship of all creative work to the ultimate source: "All productivity of the highest kind, every important conception, every discovery, every great thought which bears fruit, is in no one's control, and is beyond every earthly power. Such things are to be regarded as unexpected gifts from above, as pure divine products." Like the great poets who invoked the divine muses as the inspirers of their works, George Eliot declared that in all the writings which she considered to be her best there was a "not herself" which took possession of her and made her feel "her own personality to be merely the instrument through which the spirit acted."

From creative workers of all types Brewster Ghiselin has

gathered a series of testimonies into a monograph on *The Creative Process*. "Production by a process of conscious calculation," he writes, "seems never to occur. . . . It cannot and ought not to be rejected as impossible, but it does not fit the facts reported almost universally in every field of creative work. Not only Shelley, Blake, Ernst, Henry James and many other artists of great note or of little have described some considerable part of their invention as entirely spontaneous and involuntary—that is, automatic. Invention, automatic in this sense, is claimed also by a variety of intellectual workers, such as Spencer, Nietzsche, Sir W. Rowan Hamilton, C. F. Gauss. More or less of such automatism is reported by nearly every worker who has much to say about his processes, and no creative process has been demonstrated to be wholly free from it."

This "automatic" property must be distinguished from the trance medium who engages in "automatic" writing or talking. The creative worker is never more fully aware than when he is at the peak of creativity. He is most fully himself, yet most fully other than himself. The mysterious paradox about losing self to find it is at such times exhibited in the immediate consciousness, and the experiencer realizes that this is his finest hour in which he is participating in something awesome and holy, mysterious and beautiful, above—not beneath—reason. Such moments contain "intimations of immortality." They are enclosed within the eternal Spirit's working in creation. "One can save oneself much trouble," advises Ghiselin, "by recognizing the limitations of the will in creation. It is interesting to see how often it is repudiated as a primary instrument in much of the creative process by all kinds of artists and thinkers, from Picasso to John Dewey, a group so large and representative as to leave no doubt that agreement is general."

These words must not be taken to mean that creation requires no effort. "I have emphasized the value of understanding, discipline, and hard work in the creative process," he writes. Then he adds words so significant for the work of prayer: "High and sustained achievement demands even more, the concentration of a life."

Consider these instances of creative discovery described by a distinguished historian and archaeologist and by two eminent mathematicians.

Sir W. M. Flinders Petrie, British Egyptologist, writes: "I never try to settle a difficult matter off-hand. I first assemble the material, state the problem as definitely as possible, and, if no solution is evident, leave it alone. From time to time I may look over it to refresh my memory, but never to force a solution. After waiting days or years I suddenly feel a wish to cover it again, and then everything runs smoothly and I can write without effort. There is unconscious growth of the mind without perceptible effort in the interval."

Dr. Banesh Hoffman, Oxford mathematician and physical relativist, records his experience. "I had been attempting to work upon a problem that had puzzled me for at least two years. I made some sporadic, half-hearted calculations on odd bits of paper, but nothing came of them. In the evening I had to go to a lecture upon an entirely different subject. After the lecture and an argument with a friend about the lecture, I went to my room and decided that I would read for the rest of the evening (a book by Trotsky on Lenin), and go to bed early. I picked up some scraps of paper and straightway, without realizing that there was any difficulty in the problem, I wrote out the solution with hardly a pause. I knew somehow or other that something had solved itself at the back of my mind, but had no idea of the solution until my pencil almost automatically wrote it out. I can't remember my feeling during the hours in which I worked, being, I suppose, too absorbed in production to notice my actual surroundings. But after I had the solution down in front of me, I remember that I was elated and, though the hour was late, had no longer any desire to go to bed. I went over to the auditorium and practiced singing. There had been no conscious results until this moment."

Two paragraphs from the memoir of the celebrated French mathematician Henri Poincaré are a testimony of the highest order to unconscious elements in mathematical creation:

"It is time to penetrate deeper and to see what goes on in the very soul of the mathematician. For this, I believe, I can do best by recalling memories of my own. But I shall limit myself to telling how I wrote my first memoir on Fuchsian functions. . . . This theorem will have a barbarous name, unfamiliar to many, but that is unimportant; what is of interest for the psychologist is not the theorem but the circumstances.

"For fifteen days I strove to prove that there could not be any functions like those that I have since called Fuchsian functions. I was then very ignorant; every day I seated myself at my work table, stayed an hour or two, tried a great number of combinations, and reached no results. One evening, contrary to my custom, I drank black coffee and could not sleep. Ideas rose in crowds; I felt them collide until pairs interlocked, so to speak, making a stable combination. By the next morning I had established the existence of a class of Fuchsian functions, those which come from the hypergeometric series; I had only to write out the results, which took but a few hours."

Studies of the conditions under which such creative moments may be evoked are of great import for a modern Christian understanding of the laws of prayer. Wallas' pioneering work on creative thought, followed by Jacques Hadamard, Eliot Hutchinson, Brewster Ghiselin, and others, suggests conditions and disciplines which are parallels to the preparation for intensely creative prayer. If prayer, as we have suggested, is living at the center of the Kingdom where the Creator still works, then all instances of so-called "secular" creative work may be an intimation of what we may expect when we are overshadowed by His Holy (Whole-making) Presence. Any difference lies in the fact that the work God does in and through prayer is of a more total nature than what the poet or artist accomplishes in his compositions.

We are now in a position to state more clearly what we mean by creativity. Novelty is necessary in creation, but it is only a part. The newness must be set forth in a higher unity and integration. There is a living wholeness about a true creation. Each part draws some of its meaning from the whole, which is more than the sum of the parts. The parts are not present by simple addition, as in a heap of rubbish, but "grow" from the whole by a kind of inevitability. This is true even where the artist has written scores of alternative variations before settling on the most fitting one. Familiarity with the rejected conclusions to Beethoven's Fifth Symphony, for example, reveals the composer's sense of the tension and togetherness of the whole work which led him to conclude it as he did. The naturalness and inevitability we feel when we hear this portion of the symphony is an intuitive sense of the living wholeness of the work which is a measure of the greatness of the composer's art.

The poet Robinson Jeffers writes of this wholeness on a larger scale:

> A severed hand
> Is an ugly thing, and man disevered from the earth and stars
>   and his history . . . for contemplation or in fact . . .
> Often appears atrociously ugly. Integrity is wholeness, the
>   greatest beauty is
> Organic wholeness, the wholeness of life and things, the divine
>   beauty of the universe.

Thus, true creation always leads toward greater harmony, beauty, integration, richness, freedom in order, and wholeness.

It is from this point of view that we should consider prayer as the highest form of creation within the highest environment for creation, the Kingdom of God. Prayer is the integration of man, nature, and God in the most inclusive and perfect whole, God-united-to-His-creation. Prayer is putting oneself at the complete disposal of the supreme Will which is forever reweaving patterns of existence into the most perfect possible work of art. As the gentle-spirited Mother Juliana taught, "For he beholdeth in love and would make us partners of his good deed, and therefore he stirreth us to prayer for that which it liketh him to do."

Some experiences of creativity, however, make us hesitate to use it as a clue to the Kingdom of God. Human egocentricity is profoundly tempted to make an idol of the creative powers, to set them off from the rest of life and from God. The experience of creativity possesses such precious value and brings to the human mind such preternatural illumination that it is easy to venerate the human vessel which enjoys it. This veneration easily leads to a cult of genius. The romantic Schelling wrote of genius as "the holy eternally-creating divine power which engenders all things" breaking forth. Goethe even went so far as to identify high religion with the culturally gifted: "To whom science and art belong, also belongs religion, but he who does not have them, has he Religion?" To be sure, as the examples cited will show, creativity is an intimation of divinity, but this intimation is much clearer in the saints who were saved in humility from severing their powers from the Source. Unfortunately it is rare that the possessor of artistic or scientific "gifts" recognizes the origin of his powers and dedicates them as did Bach, to the "glory of God alone."

The shadow of the monstrous Tower of Babel darkens all our thoughts about human creation apart from God, yet our freedom always leaves the possibility that we may attempt such idolatry. God gives His gifts, but He does not prescribe their use. However, there is an inevitable degeneration of creation dissociated from its divine origin and sustaining power. It becomes sensual and demonic. In time the creative life dwindles, dabbles in the grotesque, scratches for novelty, and finally burns itself out. Upon arrival in the far country, the prodigal son in Jesus' great parable no doubt spent his time and money on the arts, but in time he descended to lechery and wine.

Instances of creation in art and science are not the Kingdom; they are intimations of it. The continuing creation of God in the Kingdom is a masterwork of integration of the physical, mental, moral, and spiritual levels of creation. Prayer is identification with the creativity of God. It is reverent participation in His everlasting work. It is living at the growing edge of the Universe, those living nodal points where the future is coming into existence. Prayer does not reverse the divine direction, but cooperates with it. It is not concerned with the rigid deposits of past growth, the bole of the tree, but with the buds and twig tips where change is encountered. We do not pray to have a thumb restored which has been amputated, though we might well pray for an infected wound to heal. And where the conditions have been right, such prayers have produced healing at so swift a rate that the casual observer might call it instantaneous. Alexis Carrel, who claims to have watched a cancerous sore shrivel to a scar in the course of a few moments, says that the healing process is just what would be observed over a much longer time if the wound had healed naturally. We do not pray for the moon and stars to change their courses, but we may well pray for those multitudinous events in which the undetermined future is yet to be made. Here we may enter the Kingdom of eternal creation.

CHAPTER 10

A Pattern

of Petition

The fundamental pattern of petition is the conscious offering of our needs and desires to God, allowing Him to purify and mature them, and then trusting Him totally with the results. The rhythm of such prayer begins with the clarifying of need and desire, continues by harmonizing that desire with God's will, and concludes by releasing the prayer into His care in an act of complete faith and personal renunciation.

CLARIFYING NEED AND DESIRE

Analyze desires and wants. At first we seem to know what we truly want. We are constantly clamoring for this or that. On closer examination we discover that most so-called wants are merely reflections of what we are expected to want—a new car, a spring dress, a college degree, and so on—and not necessarily what we want in our own souls. Our conscious wanting is closely associated with the artificial ego system described in the discussion of confession. True desire springs from the ground of real need and is a reflection of the authentic growing edge of our real selfhood. The first step in petition is to bring into awareness that level of desire.

Joanna Field, describing her own perplexities at the outset of a spiritual adventure, writes, "People say, 'Oh, be yourself at all cost,' but they don't know how difficult it is to know what your real self is." Her search for inward reality began, as is so often the case, in unhappiness. The meaninglessness of her life was pervaded, however, by a haunting feeling that there was a richness to be had if one searched where it was.

Recording in her diary the rare moments of real happiness, she noted that such joy came from deep fulfillments, not from conventional satisfactions. She then listed her "wants" and "anti-wants" and every few days tried to rate them honestly. She allowed her mind to play freely with the whole hinterland of the self. Merely conventional wishes were gradually set to one side. Self-knowledge began to emerge, and the spiritual center so long suppressed began to pierce the rigid shell. Gradually her most significant wants were lifted into consciousness and her idea of life clarified "not as the slow shaping of achievement to fit my preconceived purposes, but as the gradual discovery and growth of a purpose which I did not know."

Having been taught to seek only God's will, we may wonder whether it is proper to express strong desires in prayer. We are rightly skeptical of wishing to change His mind. But the truth is that God wants us to come before Him with our deepest longings, and being human, we cannot do otherwise. It is both false humility and false theology which urge us to appear without desire before God. He planted these deep urges within us. He made us as creatures which live by alternation between need and satisfaction. We must stand before the Face with the longings which fire us and the concerns which break our hearts. A comparison of the celebrated Fire Sermon of Gautama Buddha

and our Lord's Sermon on the Mount reveals two different
views of man's relationship to the Ultimate. The Buddha taught
that desire (*tanha*, meaning thirst) was the root of suffering
and that salvation lay in its thorough quenching. "Now this,
monks," he announced, "is the noble truth of the way that leads
to the cessation of pain, the cessation without remainder of
craving. . . ." Many mystics both from the East and West have
followed this "Path." The Christ, however, bids us not to quench
our desire but rather to purify it and then offer it to God. "Ask,
and it shall be given you; seek, and ye shall find; knock, and it
shall be opened unto you." "How much more will your Father
who is in heaven give good things to those who ask him?"
"Your heavenly Father knoweth that ye have need of all these
things."

Desire, the motive force by which life goes forward, performs
a great work in God's creation. Our deepest desires lead us
toward the Kingdom. "Follow your longing," writes Carl Jung,
"and it will lead you to God." In *The People, Yes,* Carl Sand-
burg adds:

> A tough will counts. So does desire.
> So does a rich soft wanting.
> Without rich wanting nothing arrives.

Aristotle saw all the events of nature and society as a movement
of desire awakened in things and men by the supreme attractive
power of the Unmoved Mover, God. The late Professor Bright-
man of Boston University spoke of the "dialectic of desire," by
which he sought to show that when we understand our desire in
its total context we discover that it involves God.

Prayer will be only as powerful as the desire behind it. Neu-
rotically twisted desire can produce illness in body and mind,
force events into violent patterns, and frustrate creation at
many points. On the other hand, a "rich soft wanting," which

reflects the deepest nature of a man, works great things in prayer. The ideal of petition is that every need, as it arises, be offered to God as a sacrifice of love and an expression of humble dependence.

Continue confessional prayer. It is our unreality, our ego-centricity, which blocks the life of communion with God. The prayer power of the great saints lay in their sanctity. The chief law of petition, therefore, is that we be real persons before The Person. God fortunately does not answer the ravings of our pride and the misdirected wishes of the ego. But the direct and simple offering of need by a man who has submitted to the cleansing power of God's gracious holiness has great power in heaven.

There is empirical evidence to suggest that the prayer of an inwardly divided man will be frustrated. In experimentation with extrasensory perception (ESP), for example, Professor Rhine has discovered that prejudice against ESP causes an experimental subject to miss more answers on tests than he would if he merely guessed. His score is *worse* than when answers are made by chance alone. In other words, it seems that *such a person knows the right answer and represses it.* This evidence is important, because there are a good many affinities between the conditions favorable to successful ESP performance and the conditions, such as faith, friendliness, and motivation, deemed proper for creative prayer. There appears also to be a positive relationship between good personality adjustment and high performance.

In the light of this material, we may foresee the case in which a person subconsciously refuses an answer to his conscious prayer either because he does not actually believe that prayer can be answered, or because he does not really want what he has prayed for.

In *Faith is the Answer,* Norman Vincent Peale tells of a young woman who was distressed by fears that her aging father, for whom she was keeping house, might die. In a panic of anxiety she would hurry home early from parties. Through skilled counseling she came to realize that her unconscious concern was not for her father's health, but was a profound wish that he might die and relieve her of a heavy burden.

Let us suppose that before therapy this young woman had decided to pray for her father. What kind of prayer would it have been? Her words and conscious thoughts would have been contradicted by her deep mind. Assuming that there was some energy left over from the inner conflict, what kind of influence would have flowed from her toward her father? Professor Rhine suggests that we have enough evidence to justify experimentation on the way in which ill states of mind and body may profoundly affect those closely bound to us by ties of blood or affection. Without knowing the answers to these questions, we may, nevertheless, draw a useful conclusion that it is unsafe to use petition without coupling it with spiritual growth. In fact, the more bold we are in one, the more advanced we must be in the other.

Practice wholeheartedness. Full wholeheartedness occurs on the highest levels of personality only when everything flows toward God's Kingdom. Short of that level, there are, however, moments when our whole being is caught up in the desperate need of the hour, and prayer is offered passionately to God. Such prayers are often answered. For example, men on a raft in the Pacific, who are dying for lack of food and water, offer at last the most wholehearted prayer of their lives. Strange events occur. Such a cry is not unheeded.

Some people will object. Why does God answer them? They are not better than many whose prayers languish unanswered! But the prayers of desperation were answered because of their wholeheartedness. Rarely do ordinary men come to such singlemindedness in their relationship to God. In a saint such focusing occurs as the result of long spiritual discipline, after which he experiences a continuous flow of response. The man who waits

K

until events bring him to such urgent praying as described in the raft experience is at the mercy of outward circumstance. Although he is not a model to follow, his prayer illustrates the rule.

Practice persistence. Two parables of Jesus teach persistence in prayer. We may be sure he did not mean that God was a calloused judge or a sleepy neighbor, but that through persistence before Him something essential happens to petition which is necessary to its fulfillment. Persistence forces us to test desire and to clarify it in expression. Furthermore, it tests our willingness to focus completely in concentrated awareness upon God to whom the need is offered.

Practice concentration. A scattered consciousness receives nothing. This fact is true not only in prayer, but also in other kinds of creative work. Through the sharp focus of awareness our being goes out to God, and His grace in turn flows into us. Our habitual stream of consciousness, which is choked with all sorts of debris, must turn into a deep, crystal-clear channel. The Buddha taught that in meditation the mind must cease leaping about and burn steadily like a "lamp in a windless place."

Many oddities in the history of prayer may be explained as methods designed to attain a concentrated state. Mary Austin tells us that there was among the Paiute Indians a powerful belief in the "Friend in the Soul of Man." The old chief told her that "by prayer you laid hold on it and if your prayed aright you got what you asked." However, "You didn't get help from the Friend simply by asking; you had first to get to Him or It. You had to make a veritable motion of your own soul, 'here.' (He moved his hand over the regions of his solar plexus.) When you had climbed up to the Friend by rhythmic motions and noises you laid hands on Him, and the thing you wanted happened."

Mary Austin speculates that rhythmic movements and sounds

break the spell of immediate circumstances and their hold on attention, and thus allow consciousness to be filled exclusively with an awareness of the Friend and the hoped-for boon.

Many devices—fasting, watching (going without sleep), drugs, beatings, painful postures, and breathing exercises—have been used to augment concentration. Because such methods may be dangerous, it is wiser to use moderate physical disciplines, together with patient and persistent practice in holding the attention firm. Each person must develop his own methods, but Miss Austin is correct in pointing out that "everybody lives more or less in a coil of immediate claims upon attention which must be shuffled off before the attention can be effectively fixed on the creative principle which it is its design to use as a basis of prayer."

Develop willingness to act in accordance with our petitions. Action is a great purifier of desire. A test of sincerity is our preparation to act in accordance with our petition. If, for example, I pray for health and refuse to obey the known laws of health, my will is not unified and my desire for health is not deep enough to be honored by God. Or if I pray for money and persistently fail to use my present resources, then my willing is chaotic and contradictory and is no true prayer.

Clarify the object desired. Desire always seeks an object of corresponding satisfaction in the outer world. When we hunger or thirst, we find relief through eating and drinking. To pray well we must be wise concerning facts and values which are authentically satisfying to a real person. Such wisdom aids immeasurably in the directing of desire toward its proper object. A man may re-educate a corrupted palate by habitually eating nutritious foods. So can our longings be directed toward genuine rather than spurious goods. When we pray for something that we greatly desire, we are wise to analyze dispassionately the values involved.

To illustrate this principle, let us imagine a poor student who discovers that he has not enough money to continue his education. Should he pray for funds? Certainly his need is real. Furthermore, the purpose is a good one. We may grant that he should pray, but how?

He would do well to think hard about the values he seeks through such a request—a college education, desirable social contacts, the means for personal development, the possibility of contributing eventually to the store of human knowledge, the chance to serve mankind through a useful lifework. As this search is pressed, the most fundamental values emerge. They will become the very essence of his prayer. The money is merely a means.

Praying in this manner accomplishes two things: it clarifies the supplicant's final goals and shows him wherein he has failed to use his opportunities, and it brings a sure response from God. A prayer so wise and true to man's longings cannot fail.

HARMONIZING OUR DESIRE WITH GOD'S WILL

The assumption underlying the first phase of petition, clarifying need and desire, is that if we find our deepest selves and our most fundamental desires, they will lead us to God in a unique way. Now we must consider that it is useless and presumptuous to pray for something God does not will. We now directly ask the question, Does God want what we are praying for?

A condition is always implied in the Lord's promises of answered prayer: "If ye shall ask anything *in my name*, I will do it." "Whatsoever ye shall ask of the Father *in my name*, he may give it you." "*If ye abide in me, and my words abide in you*, ye shall ask what ye will, and it shall be done unto you." "*Seek ye first the kingdom of God, and his righteousness*; and all these things shall be added unto you." That nothing can be sought in prayer which is known to be out of harmony with the divine will is an absolute law. Who can pray, then, except the man who seeks in every way to discover what the divine will is for him? This means to saturate oneself with a deep knowledge of Jesus Christ, to come in every way possible to a comprehension of his Kingdom, and gradually to bend stubborn self-will to a posture of humble obedience.

This absolute priority of God's will in prayer does not absolve us from finding our own will. God's will is particular for us in the details of our lives. We cannot learn to pray simply in general terms. God is love, but how and where that love enters our lives is something we can find only through knowing ourselves as well as Him. If we can keep both our clarified need and God's holy will in equal focus, our prayer will have depth and reality. We must know our soul's sincere desire clearly and then set it in the framework of the Kingdom.

Setting human longing in the framework of the Kingdom saves prayer from the taint of magic, the art which seeks to coerce God to do man's will. Because petition has often been suspected of being a thinly veiled practice of magical art, many sensitive spirits have given it up. In one of the tales of the Hasidim the disciple of a very holy rabbi rebukes the disciple of another, saying, "You regard it as a miracle when God does the will of your Rabbi; we regard it as indeed a miracle when it can be truly said that our Rabbi has done the will of God."

But it should be pointed out that the will of God may be that our prayer shall be effective for a real difference in events and life, though, of course, a difference which God Himself wants. Because He creates in part through us, He does not demand that we be desireless or have no will, but that we sanctify our desires and yield our will to Him.

How these two wills—mine and God's—can flow together in prayer was answered five hundred years ago in the words of

Mother Juliana of Norwich. God, in His loving revelations, said
to her:

> I am the Ground of thy beseeching:
> First it is my will that thou have it;
> And after I make thee to will it;
> And since, I make thee to beseech it
> And thou beseechest it,
> How should it then be that thou shouldst not have
>   thy beseeching?

In satisfying this second condition of prayer, harmony with
the divine will, a serious man will formulate "Kingdom tests"
for his petitions. Tests suggested by an understanding of the
work of confession and the first phase of petition are implied in
such questions as: Is it a real need or merely an expression of
ego pride? Is it an escape from the consequences of sins we
refuse to submit to God's surgery? Is it an expression of fear,
envy, greed, or inferiority? Tests suggested by an understanding
of the goals of Christian maturity and the nature of God's
Kingdom are found in these questions: Is it the prayer of a real
self to the real God? Is it loving and honest? Is it the most
inclusive good possible at this time? Is it in harmony with the
lifework to which God has called me? Tests are also suggested
by these great passages of Scripture: Paul's description of the
Christian life, Romans 12; the dimensions of Christian love,
1 Corinthians 13; the fruits of the spirit, Galatians 5:22 ff.;
Philippians 4:8; Ephesians 4:13-15; and the Sermon on the
Mount, Matthew 5.

RELEASING PRAYER INTO HIS CARE

Having clarified need and desire and having harmonized them
both with God's will, we must now release the petition into
His care. We are ready for two profound spiritual acts: *An act*

of faith and *an act of complete renunciation.* The first is an affirmation of our trust in God; the second is a complete giving of ourselves to Him.

An act of faith. Petition that begins with need but does not end in complete trust in God is a cry, but not a prayer. Complete confidence in God is what Jesus called *faith,* and he made it the condition of power in petition. "Whatever you ask in prayer, believe that you receive it, and you will." "All things are possible to him who believes."

Trusting God with our deepest desires in prayer means more than hoping against hope. "The faith that shuts the mouths of lions," as Glenn Clark has pointed out, "is more than a pious hope that they will not bite." Our faith must be equal to or greater than the urgent need which led to prayer. The fear or revulsion created by disease or sin must be matched by a confidence and love which flows from the knowledge that God is able and willing to overcome any evil.

The whole mood of petition is changed as we look from our needs or desire to God. Then not *asking,* but what Emerson calls "glad conspiring reception," takes possession. If our prayer truly reflects God's will, He desires our prayer even more than our feeble longing can appreciate. He loves us, His children, far more than we love ourselves. His concern is to relieve us of sin, sickness, or sorrow, and to supply us with all we need to live fully and richly within the Kingdom which it is His good pleasure to give.

When united to Christ and his wisdom, our prayer has the same power he exhibited in the days of his flesh. We are no longer servants, but friends and God's sons. "All things are yours; . . . and you are Christ's; and Christ is God's."

But it may be asked, What can I do to get the faith which prayer requires? This perplexing and important question may be answered with the following practical suggestions:

Understand the nature of prayer and its mode of co-operation with God. Many times our faith is hindered by a false view of God, prayer, and our co-operation with Him. This view may be either infantile or highly sophisticated, but it is an effective block in either case. This book attempts to make clear the kind of universe in which prayer succeeds and is intended as an aid to intelligent faith.

Memorize and affirm great Biblical passages which undergird faith. Several examples are: "In everything God works for good with those who love him." "I have loved thee with an everlasting love: therefore with loving-kindness have I drawn thee." "Bless the Lord, O my soul, and forget not all his benefits, who forgives all your iniquity, who heals all your diseases, who redeems your life from the Pit, who crowns you with steadfast love and mercy, who satisfies you with good as long as you live." "Behold, I am the Lord, the God of all flesh; is anything too hard for me?" Each person will find those passages which speak to his condition.

A helpful exercise is to paraphrase Biblical language by using first personal pronouns, in this manner: "My faith is the substance of that which I long for; my desire is the forerunner of the finished work." "Even now as I pray I believe that I have received what I have asked God for." "I have this confidence in Jesus, that whatever I ask God for in his spirit He hears and answers me." "O Lord, thou art in this very problem which confronts me working for good in it."

Learn the faith-building power of parable, analogy, and verbal symbols. Glenn Clark refers to "handles of power" which are personal experiences through which we grasp God's intention. The centurion, because he was a man of authority, for example, had confidence in the authority of Jesus. Clark reports that he was able to look from the body of a girl terribly broken in an automobile accident to the perfection of God and the certainty of His care, because he remembered that before the accident she had made an appointment with him to discuss the spiritual life. Such appointments, he reflected, like that of Jesus and his disciples to meet after his death in Galilee, are made in eternity and cannot be broken. Such is a "handle of power." The parabolic consciousness which weaves meaning out of the texture of our particular situation leads to faith.

Joanna Field recounts that in her spiritual pilgrimage there came to her quite by accident a realization of the power of words to change and focus inner events. Prayer is not "much speaking," but words often function powerfully in our consciousness. It is wisdom to remember phrases which stir the deepest levels of the subconscious and bring into awareness a heavy freight of meaning that leads to faith. Hindu teachers, justifying the constant use of the word "Om" in meditation, claim that the mere mention of the word arouses and compresses into a moment the faith and aspiration of a lifetime of meditation.

Psychology and semantics give support to this practice. The psychoanalyst watches for single words or phrases which are significant to the patient. In recent experiments a new "feed-back" method proved successful with subjects who had previously resisted hypnosis. The method consists simply in asking subjects to record their feelings during unsuccessful attempts. The words and phrases used in these descriptions are then employed by the hypnotist when a fresh attempt is made. When the right words are used, success follows.

Semantics, the science which examines the relationship of language to reality, has many things to say concerning the use of language to arouse feeling and control behavior. An impressive body of the data that has been accumulated is of use to those who would learn to pray. First, it suggests that proper use of words may control and direct deep feelings and attitudes. It, furthermore, gives us a clue to many of our Reality-avoiding

responses, such as prejudices, fears, or irritations. To a certain
extent we may say, control the words and you control the
response.

Recall previous answers to prayer. Often in the urgency of
need or concern there come flashes of doubt or brief eclipses
of faith. The problem looms so large that we forget that God is
still running the universe. At such a moment we may recover our
assurance by recollecting God's previous loving kindness to us
and others. The testimony of the past has a powerful ministry
to perform in us if we would only stop to remember. When the
children of Israel were in doubt of their future, Moses restored
their faith by reviving their memories. "Ask now of the days
that are past."

Practice positive picturing. Imagination is a great mystery. It
may lead either to illusion or reality, even though the common
opinion is that the "world of the imagination" is pure fancy. In
prayer, this faculty is put at the service of God and serves as a
link to His supreme or creative Power. In the first phase of petition detailed picturing clarifies need. In the second phase it
clarifies the nature of the answer. In the third phase such picturing overcomes the obsessive fear and fascination with evil which
interfere with our joyful surrender and serves also as the channel
through which a divine response comes.

To serve these purposes the picturing power must be rendered
sensitive to different levels of reality. It must first of all be sensitive of our own inner life. The imagination is often infected with
alien images imposed from the outside. Then, it must become
sensitive to the "growing edge" of events and have prophetic
power to cast up into consciousness a glimpse of events not yet
born. The purpose of such insight is not to predict the future but
to co-operate with the inner tendency and bent of things toward
completeness. If we take seriously St. Paul's words that "God
works in everything," then we may add that the dedicated im-

agination perceives His will for each unfolding occasion. Here, as Shakespeare says, "imagination bodies forth the form of things unknown," but God, not the poet's pen,

> Turns them to shapes, and gives to airy nothing
> A local habitation and a name.

The highest level of reality to which imagination must be sensitive is the inclusive Kingdom. Here the vision of good is so overwhelming that even in the midst of the most insistent need, we rejoice because of the glorious fulfillment which is even now "in our midst" and which is at this moment "coming among us."

When the imagination has this depth, it gives great power in prayer. On the other hand, I have known people in trouble who did not ask their Christian friends to pray for them because they feared the effects of negative sympathy. ("Isn't it too bad about so-and-so? I wonder how the poor fellow is getting on.") Much praying fails and may even have bad effects, because the imagination is chained to negative pictures of illness and suffering. A woman of great wisdom in prayer tells us that her prayer group was failing to help a desperately ill friend. Failing to understand the reason, she talked with one well-seasoned in this work and received this counsel: "You're seeing her sick, my dear. You'll have to see her well."

Some years ago Glenn Clark discovered that answers to prayer seemed to depend not so much upon the way petitions are offered as on the state of consciousness which emerged in the course of praying. The moment of deep peace and trust, joyful confidence, or positive visioning seemed to be the crucial turning point in events. When faith, love, and joy turned into knowledge, oneness, and bliss, he "knew" the thing for which he prayed was at that moment coming to pass. This "spiritualized consciousness" is not merely a state of feeling; it is a moment in which, doubts and fears aside, a person wholly focuses upon God and knows the fullness of His answering love.

An act of complete renunciation. With this understanding we turn to the final phase of petition, the complete giving of ourselves to Him. We must not only release our prayer in faith; we must also renounce all claims in an act of humility. Gandhi's favorite verse of scripture, the opening words of the *Isha Upanishad,* proclaimed this truth: "The whole world is the garment of the Lord. Renounce it, then, and receive it back as a gift of God." The spiritual rhythm of asking all, yet renouncing and giving all, produced in his life consequences which the most irresponsible dreamer could not have envisaged.

We must trust in God's own way of dealing with our needs. We may begin as did Jesus in the Garden of Olivet where he prayed three times, "Remove this cup from me." But in the end there must come complete renunciation and submission to the Will. He may deny our petition in favor of some more costly though more redemptive answer. Jesus' surrender meant crucifixion and resurrection. For us—it is up to God.

In all types of prayer we come time and again to the necessity for a deeper commitment and self-offering until the whole of our life and interests is laid upon the altar of God. We discover that a great mystery is to be found in the twofold movement of renunciation and grace. By giving all, we receive all. St. John of the Cross wrote: "That thou mayest have pleasure in everything, seek to know nothing. That thou mayest possess all things, seek to possess nothing." "The Kingdom of God," Eckhart says, "belongs only to the thoroughly dead." The Third Patriarch of Zen expressed the wisdom of this abandonment of self-will in spiritual affairs with these words:

> The Great Way is no harder than men themselves
> Make it by not refusing to prefer;
> For where there is no abhorrence, where there is no
> Frenzy to have, the Way lies manifest.

Jesus summarizes with the sweeping demand, "Whoever loses his life for my sake will find it."

In his analysis of the healing at Lourdes, described in Chapter 9, Dr. Blanton points out that the patient was at the end of his rope. He was ready to give up. In fact, all the healings recorded by the Medical Bureau at Lourdes were of cases *in extremis*. Apparently, when men suffer what they can bear, they bear it alone, but when they have passed beyond their strength and throw themselves without reserve upon God, miracles take place.

A friend confides that when he prays in his church he kneels only on one knee. One knee represents his acknowledgment of God's right; the other represents his freedom and independence. Such an attitude completely misunderstands the relationship between God and the soul. Our freedom is rooted in our total surrender. The Will to which we yield in prayer is not merely a superwill or some overwhelming power which overrules and overrides us. Rather from His Will our own will draws strength to be itself, much as the eating of food which comes from outside the body does not decrease the body's independence and power, but enhances it. When we understand this, we see that all our refusal to submit to God is mere rationalization. Our refusal to withdraw from other gods is what keeps the soul in bondage.

How complete should this submission be? The following story may answer this question: "Rabbi Meir sat during the whole of the Sabbath day in the School instructing the people. During his absence from the house his two sons died, both of them of uncommon beauty and enlightened in the Law. His wife bore them to her bed-chamber, and spread a white covering over their bodies. In the evening Rabbi Meir came home. 'Where are my sons?' he asked. 'I repeatedly looked round the School, and I did not see them there.' She reached him a goblet. He praised the Lord at the going out of the Sabbath, drank, and again asked,

'Where are my sons?' 'They will not be afar off,' she said, and
placed food before him that he might eat. When he had said
grace after the meal, she thus addressed him: 'With thy permission, I would fain propose to thee one question.' 'Ask it then,' he
replied. 'A few days ago a person entrusted some jewels into
my custody, and now he demands them of me; should I give
them back again?' 'This is a question,' said the Rabbi, 'which my
wife should not have thought it necessary to ask. What! Wouldst
thou hesitate to restore to everyone his own?' 'No,' she replied;
'but yet I thought it best not to restore them without acquaint-
ing you therewith.' She then led him to the chamber, and took
the white covering from the dead bodies. 'Ah, my sons! my
sons!' loudly lamented the father. 'My sons! the light of my eyes!'
The mother turned away and wept bitterly. At length she took
her husband by the hand, and said, 'Didst thou not teach that we
must not be reluctant to restore that which was entrusted to our
keeping? See—the Lord gave, and the Lord hath taken away;
blessed be the name of the Lord.' "

Rudolph Otto in his *Idea of the Holy* recounts Max Eyth's
story of the building of the mighty bridge over the estuary of
the Ennobucht. "The most profound and thorough labour of
the intellect," he writes, "the most assiduous and devoted professional toil, had gone to the construction of the great edifice,
making it in all its significance and purposefulness a marvel of
human achievement. In spite of endless difficulties and gigantic
obstacles, the bridge is at length finished, and stands defying
wind and waves. Then there comes a raging cyclone, and the
building and builder are swept into the deep. Utter meaninglessness seems to triumph over the richest significance, blind 'destiny'
seems to stride on its way over prostrate virtue and merit. The
narrator tells how he visits the scene of the tragedy and returns
again. 'When we got to the end of the bridge, there was hardly
a breath of wind; high above, the sky showed blue-green and

with an eerie brightness. Behind us, like a great open grave lay the Ennobucht. The Lord of life and death hovered over the waters in silent majesty. We felt his presence, as one feels one's own hand. And the old man and I knelt down before the open grave and before Him.' "

This total submission before God seems quite contrary to the modern mood. We do not understand or approve this final submission before the awesome grandeur of God. We wish to claim our right to challenge or even to defy Him. We spurn this renunciation and submission as a false fatalism or a contemptible decay of personal self-respect. We cannot understand and accept this except through prolonged experience in prayer. In the constant encounter with God we learn that we have nothing to fear in such total self-giving, for He is our true home, the dwelling place of the soul. We may not understand all that happens to us, but we may know a profound trust that affirms with Socrates on trial for his life: "No evil can happen to a good man either in life or after death."

In the prayer of petition all the moods of prayer seem to coalesce. All praying, even this which seeks to transform events, becomes essentially an oblation and a sacrifice. Evelyn Underhill has written that this "free self-offering without condition to the transforming energy of God—the oblation of the natural life with all its gifts, possessions and capacities . . . is at once an adoration, an intercession, and a sacrifice."

CHAPTER II

Enlarging the Circle

of Grace Through Intercession

In intercession we rise to the highest plane of the Christian life, because God, my fellow human beings, and I are gathered into a loving unity of need and satisfaction. St. Paul writes that the Spirit itself joins our intercessions and participates on both the hither as well as the Other side of the human-divine relationship. "The Spirit itself maketh intercession for us with groanings which cannot be uttered."

Some treatises on prayer favor contemplation over intercession as a purer form of devotion. But contemplation that does not contain intercessory elements, that does not include one's fellow human beings, is fragmentary and abstracted from the living incarnational Whole of God-united-to-His-creation. In the teaching of Jesus, reverence and love, devotion and compassion are always related. Much of Jesus' instruction seems strikingly unreligious, for it is directed mostly to the adjustment of living relationships and deals with anger, deceit, or anxiety. If we would enter into loving communion with God, He reminds us to uproot bitterness, resentment, or jealousy and make peace with our brother. Apparently reverence toward God and love toward men are inseparably joined. The God-denying humanist and the world-denying mystic strive to separate what God has joined together.

The view that prayer advances from petition through intercession to rest at last in contemplation alone is, in my opinion, unjustified. In the total context of living relationship we never cease petition—bringing all our needs and satisfactions in loving trust of God—or intercession—entering into direct spiritual relationship with our fellow man through his needs in actual situations—or communion—the constant awareness of the surrounding Presence of the transcendent-immanent God who "so loved the world that He gave His Son."

E. Herman, the author of *Creative Prayer*, teaches two forms of intercession: prophetic intercession which is concerned with specific situations and persons; and priestly intercession which lifts hands of prayer for "all sorts and conditions of men." Prophetic intercession should lead at last to a moment of general compassion and high faith wherein all human needs are lifted into the Presence. Continuing year after year in the priestly act of general intercession is difficult, but I am convinced with E. Herman that the whole climate of our earthly life is sweetened and cleansed by the silent work of the unnamed saints who through prayer have offered faith and love to all living beings.

THE FOUNDATION FOR INTERCESSION

One of the persistent psychological obstacles to a life of intercession is the common-sense conviction that we are separated absolutely from our fellows in much the way that the planets are separated from the sun and from one another. But in the spiritual realm space means nothing. The "I" that is behind my brain is not at any "place" which can be designated. Thoughts and

L

values are not in space, unless we are willing to speak of social space or personal space. To pray for a friend on another continent is as fruitful as to pray for a person in the next room. All of us have a kind of co-presence in God. In His Being we are intimately connected and have our true relationship with one another.

Certain trends in recent research and reflection reinforce very substantially this conviction of human unity from which the life of intercession springs. First, there is the new concept of man in the social sciences. The older attempts to explain man by analyzing him into atomistic elements is giving way to a "field" approach in which man is seen in the total setting of society and nature. The idea of an isolated personality is regarded as romantically absurd. At the deepest levels of their personalities men are participants in the family, class, society and civilization of their time. The whole person is involved in the total situation to which he responds at all levels of his being.

Second, the new developments in natural science, some of which are outlined in Chapter 2, support Alfred North Whitehead's criticism of the Newtonian notion of "simple location," the idea that physical objects have a definite and isolated place in absolute space. In the new science a physical object is defined as a field of force within progressively larger fields of force. According to Whitehead, every particle of matter is affected by every other particle throughout the entire reach of space-time.

Third, the twentieth-century "philosophy of organism," the philosophy that reality is a living whole, has been developed by the most distinguished thinkers: Bergson, Dreisch, Whitehead, Smuts, Hartshorne, Ferré, and Heim, to name a few. These fascinating speculations constitute further important testimony on behalf of human unity.

Fourth, important support comes from research into *Psi* phenomena (telepathy, clairvoyance, and psychokinesis), especially the work of Professors Rhine and Thouless. The careful student will wish to examine the experimental evidence reported in the *Journal of Para-Psychology*, edited by J. B. Rhine, and in the *Proceedings for the Society for Physical Research* (English). Three excellent summaries are to be found in J. B. Rhine, *Reach of the Mind*; Raynor Johnson, *The Hidden Splendor*; and G. N. Tyrrel, *The Personality of Man*. Two reliable books that report significant experiments by the authors themselves are Wilkins and Sherman, *Thoughts through Space*, and Upton Sinclair, *Mental Radio*. The existence of *Psi* faculties is nearly unanimously conceded by those who have examined the evidence. Present research is engaged in determining the laws which control these phenomena.

Both the existence and nature of such powers have a bearing on intercession. We are apparently in touch telepathically with other minds all the time, even when we are unaware of it. Furthermore, such contact is unaffected by space. Rhine writes: "Extrasensory perception has succeeded over distances as great as four thousand miles. . . . Tests made at a distance of two hundred miles and two feet showed no significant difference in results."

Such contact, though unaffected by distance, varies according to the emotional or blood ties of the persons involved. This interpersonal connection rises into awareness, however, only under certain conditions, some of which are physical. Drugs and fatigue, for example, affect it. Other conditions are psychological, including confidence, emotional calm, and happiness.

This total development of thought along many fronts assures us that we belong to one another in God and that our separateness, not our individuality, is somehow an illusion created by sin and ignorance. The problem of intercession, we now see, is not to make some connection with the person for whom we would pray, but to hallow and use the channels already there. We need not persuade a remote God to change the circumstances or character of another who is also remote. We need rather to unblock those deep channels of interconnection and let the eternal life flow in continuous streams of living water.

"The point was illustrated for me," writes Leslie D. Weatherhead, "when I recalled two farmers in India, both of whom sank wells on their separated land, only to find that underneath both farms was a great underground lake. If A had put a sack of arsenic into his well, he would have poisoned the water which B drank. If he had put—for the sake of illustration—some health-giving salt or vitamin into his own well, he would have improved the water for B also. The illustration goes a long way. To sin is to poison the public reservoir. To love is to strengthen the whole community. When A prays for B he does not, as it were, make a ball of prayer, throw it up to God and ask God to throw it down to B with greater force. He is himself in contact with B, and both are 'in God.' "

SOME RESULTS OF INTERCESSION

There are three types of results which follow from the skilled practice of intercession. First, there are the changes, healings, conversion, and reconciliations which take place in those for whom the prayers are offered. To illustrate this healing, Leslie Weatherhead draws upon the experience of Dr. Howard Somervell, Fellow of the Royal College of Surgeons, and member of the Mount Everest Expedition (1922), one of the five to reach the 28,000-foot level. In his book, *After Everest,* Somervell tells of a schoolmaster afflicted with tuberculosis of the bone: "The disease is one which medical science reckons to be well-nigh incurable when it has reached this stage. The man was going down hill and daily getting weaker and more feverish. His legs became more and more painful; and after a few weeks we took another X-ray picture and found the disease was worse in that the whole of the bone was involved. There was only one thing to do, and that was to amputate the leg to save the patient's life."

Having sent his diagnosis and the X-ray to India's greatest authority on bone disease, he received a reply. "His answer was just as we had expected. The disease was tubercular, and the only chance of saving the man's life was to take off his leg at the knee. So we told the poor fellow that there was nothing else to be done. His reply was unexpected: 'Will you give me three weeks? I want to try the effect of praying about it.' We agreed to give him that time, and the next day he went home. In three weeks he turned up true to his promise. He had left the hospital feverish, ill, flushed in the face, and only capable of being carried about. He returned in a car, but hobbling with a stick and looking much better. The wound in the leg was not healed, but the leg itself, as revealed by the X-rays, was wonderfully improved, though not yet free from the disease.

"We were amazed. What had he done to make so great an improvement? He told us quite simply that he had been quite sure it was against the will of God for any of His servants to suffer, and that he had before him a life of service to God if only he could keep his leg and his life. So he called his family and friends together and said to them, 'Look here, will you folk unite in prayer for this leg of mine that it be completely healed?' They agreed, and for a week a continuous chain of prayer was kept up by that family. One of them would pray for a quarter of an hour. Then another would take it up, and so on for over a week. In another three weeks he came to see us again. The leg had healed. He was able to walk on it and appeared almost well. A few months later he was back at school, perfectly fit, playing games with the boys, running about on both legs with no sign of disease."

Second, there are changes which take place in the person who prays. There is a gradual though perceptible deepening of character. A physical disability is often healed as the person prays for someone else. Mary Austin records that she arranged a trip to

Italy for what the doctors said would be the last year of her life. She was suffering from cancer of the breast. Her "breath drawn tight against pain," she went from church to church where she practiced the art of prayer which she long since had mastered. She did not pray for herself but for the preservation of the folk art of the American Indians, among whom she had labored most of her life, and for the people who would have to carry on the work left undone by her anticipated death. One day in Venice she met a friend who inquired concerning her health. Suddenly she became aware that she could not remember where she had left the sling given her by the doctor. Cautiously, she felt her breast. There was no pain. Later the medical examiner pronounced her cured.

The third consequence of intercession is a growing awareness of the spiritual world. "We know that we have passed out of death into life, because we love the brethren," writes St. John. Such knowledge has been thought to be the exclusive possession of the mystic who has passed into ecstatic contemplation. We discover that prayer for others is an intimate participation in the life of God. We "know" Him with our whole being as we flow with His healing tides. St. Paul, ecstatic though he was, proclaims that the knowledge of God comes chiefly not through mystical contemplation but through faith, love, and obedience.

SOME RULES OF INTERCESSION

The conditions of intercession are fundamentally the same as those which govern petition. Nevertheless, in this new enterprise of prayer the perspective changes somewhat, leading to a different formulation. There are six rules the progressive satisfaction of which lead on to great effectiveness in intercession.

The rule of love. We pray best when the inner pain suffered by others becomes lodged in our consciousness as our own. The disciples of Sri Ramakrishna, a nineteenth-century Hindu ascetic, claimed that when the saint saw a man beaten, red welts appeared on his own back. Sensitive counselors have testified that they have often been swept by unaccountable emotions of fear or hostility which they recognized later to be the inner life of the patient registering on themselves. If this deep sympathy is missing we lack genuine longing for the welfare of others. Intercession then becomes merely a matter of words and phrases. But when love deepens us, the needs of others become mixed up with our own being, their troubles become the agonizing longing of our own souls, and we are ready to pray out of the depths.

The rule of vicarious suffering. This carries the law of love even further. Evelyn Underhill, whose skill in distilling the wisdom of the saints guides us here as in so many other places, has written: "We are far from realizing all that human spirits can do for one another on spiritual levels if they will pay the price; how truly and really our souls interpenetrate, and how impossible and unChristian it is to 'keep ourselves to ourselves.' When St. Catherine of Siena used to say to the sinners who came to her: 'Have no fear, I will take the burden of your sins,' she made a practical promise, which she fulfilled literally and at her own great cost. She could do this because she was totally self-given to the purpose of the Spirit, was possessed by the Divine passion of saving love, and so had taken her place in the great army of rescuing souls.

" 'You will never do much for people, except by suffering for them,' said the Abbé Huvelin. . . . Real intercession is a form of sacrifice; and sacrifice always costs something; always means suffering, even though the most deeply satisfying joy of which we are capable is mingled with its pain. . . . When they [the saints] find someone struggling with temptation, or persisting in wrongdoing, or placed in a great spiritual danger, they are moved to a passionate and unconditional self-offering on that person's behalf."

The rule of faith. The unconditional sympathy and love re-

quired by the two foregoing rules are dangerous unless supple-
mented by an equal faith. A sensitive person may be sucked into a
whirlpool of pain and despair and become helpless as the person
whom he would help. Deep faith, an unconditional confidence in
the intention and power of God to redeem man from his trouble,
allows us to come into the orbit of suffering with a redemptive
answer. The more sensitive one is to evil, the more he must come
to know with certainty the saving Power. Our model is Jesus
who, though he wept at the tomb of his friend Lazarus, had a
faith greater than the surrounding sorrow.

Some years ago I visited a dear friend who was a patient in a
tuberculosis sanatorium. During the first visits I was so afflicted
by sympathetic pains in the chest that I almost questioned my
own health. The remedy was to spend a half hour in positive
mental prayer before entering the hospital in order that I might
keep a vision of health and power uppermost.

The rule of persistence. Often we lose the battle for someone's
welfare because we do not continue to pray after the initial and
often dramatic events seem to indicate the desired change. Re-
cently our community was shaken by the death of a boy who had
been thought healed by prayer. The community was first drawn
to pray for him when it appeared he would die of leukemia. After
the prayers, he miraculously recovered. Laboratory tests failed to
reveal any further traces of the disease. Though still in a
weakened condition, he returned to school. In about six months,
however, he was ill again. Again the community prayed. After
this he recovered so strikingly that he took a summer job and in
the fall returned to school. By mid-October he was dead. My own
judgment is that if we had been able to carry that boy in uninterrupted prayer for two or three years he would have recovered
permanently.

We cease praying too soon. The surgical technique for internal
cancer now calls for an exploratory operation six months after

the initial surgery and before further symptoms would normally appear. If possible, remaining cancerous tissue is then removed. Other exploration continues at six-month intervals until at last no traces of the disease are found. Christian patience in prayer requires that we be as thorough as that.

The rule of praying for the whole person. We are tempted to pray for the removal of annoying or disabling symptoms rather than the roots of the trouble. A woman of the Divine Science faith told me of a neighbor who was at her wit's end because of her husband's drinking habits. They proposed to remedy the situation by prayer. Each morning, when the husband had left the house, the two women sat in concentrated meditation. They pictured the man as cured of any desire to drink. Three weeks passed, and then one day the man said to his wife: "I feel very strange. I've completely lost any desire to drink." The months that followed seemed to prove that he had spoken the truth.

Six months later, following a bitter quarrel, the wife said, "I suppose you're going out to get drunk." And he did!

These women had concentrated upon a symptom and left the underlying domestic relationship untouched.

The same error is often committed in medicine, social work, and even psychiatry. The disabling symptoms are removed, but the underlying causes are uncured. Intercession must lift the whole person and all his relationships into the Kingdom. If the person is close to us, this often requires profound changes in ourselves as the new Reality of love reorders the whole of life.

This necessity is reinforced by the growing field of psychiatric knowledge. It now appears possible that nearly every illness, neurosis, accident, or outward circumstance has a "meaning" which compels the sufferer to perpetuate his trouble in answer to some deep need. He may long for a vacation which he cannot justify; the illness "forces" it upon him. He may wish to change vocations but fears to take the jump; hence accidents begin to multiply. He may resent his aging parents and the care they require, although he is unable to admit this to himself; his solicitude assumes neurotic proportions, and fear and abnormal anxiety for their health follow.

Localized trouble must be prayed for in the context of the whole good of the Kingdom where man may be healed of the ills whose roots lie in the spiritual plane.

The rule of continuing spiritual growth. When human life approaches the "maturity that is in Christ," then intercession attains its mightiest achievements. The saints, for whom God's will is supreme, are the powerhouse of prayer. Through years of spiritual growth they have been invested with the faith, hope, and love, the holiness, humility, and joy out of which God's answering response flows. The person who would practice the ministry of intercession must, for this reason, return again and again to the work of confession in which the will is recentered, and all the scattered impulses are refocused on Him.

SOME QUESTIONS ON INTERCESSION

We would be foolish to pray for something God did not will. But, if He wills it, why need we pray for it? What would we think of a farmer who says, "If it is God's will to have a crop, let Him plant and cultivate it," or of a teacher who says, "If God wants young people to acquire knowledge, let Him give it to them Himself," or of a mother who looks at her sick child and says, "Surely if God wants him well, he will recover, and so I need not give him medicine the doctor has prescribed?"

How absurd such persons would be! We know that food, knowledge, and health are things which God wills for His children, but He wills that they come through human co-operation with His laws. Let us apply this to prayer. Suppose a mother were to say, "My child is desperately ill, but I need not pray because I know that God wills health for him." Is it not as foolish to administer medicine without prayer as to offer prayers without medicine? Are they not both means of co-operation with the will of God in the given situation?

We do not understand all the laws which operate in this mysterious universe, but there is apparently one which applies to the achievement of every great good. It was formulated by St. Augustine: "Without God we cannot; without us God will not."

There is another question: Is not intercession for another, especially in the realm of character or personal habits, an invasion of the sacred freedom of the individual's personality? Is it not like a subtle type of hypnosis or strong suggestion which takes away the power of personal judgment and responsibility? The kind of prayer used by the two women to cure a drinking habit verges on an unjustifiable coercion. We saw its evil consequences. However, true loving intercession, in which the whole person and his need is lifted to the Father in faith and trust, is probably the least coercive influence one person can bring to bear on another. Like love or reason, it does not coerce but rather awakens the centers of personal responsibility and strengthens the inner will so that the recipient is more, not less, a free man.

This may be easier to see if we think of the effects of mature love upon a child. Deprive a child of such love and he will begin to have fits of anger, sulkiness, bed-wetting, attacks upon other children, and so on. Surround him with the love of mature parents, and he is released to attend freely to the world outside himself. He can learn again to make reasonable judgments, to co-operate with other children, and in many ways to manifest the powers of human freedom. In this respect love is like prayer. They may be aspects of each other. For the highest form of love is to love another as God loves him and to see him in the Kingdom of God with all his possibilities unfolding. This is also the perspective of prayer.

There may be times when the true self of one person lives in
the love and faith of another. For years Augustine wandered far
from his true self, but all the time his same true self lived in the
prayers of his mother who continuously lifted him up to God.
Peer Gynt, after a lifetime of ruinously selfish exploits, cries out:
"Where was I, as myself, as the whole man, the true man? Where
was I, with God's sigil upon my brow?" And Solveig, the woman
who has loved and prayed for him during the long absence,
answers, "In my faith, in my hope, and in my love."

SOME WAYS OF INTERCESSION

What are the ways by which we may embody these principles
in our devotional life? One proven way follows these steps:

General preparation. This preparation is fully delineated in the
descriptions of problem-solving prayer and mental prayer, so
that here it is only necessary to indicate that we must relax, surrender our own efforts into God's hands, and make an inner
declaration of intention to pray.

Meditation upon God. Two truths which we need to repeat
until they become flaming convictions are that God is able and
that God is willing. When we become seasoned in prayer, we
shall discover those reflections which convince us afresh of God's
sovereign love. We may recall past graces in prayer either known
personally to us or reported by those whom we trust. We may
meditate upon the creation as the token of God's unlimited crea-
tiveness and resourcefulness. We may find scenes from the
Gospels that remind us of God's presence both as a healing power
and outpouring grace. We wait the intuitive moment of utter
confidence in His ability to govern the world in every detail,
and of utter certainty in His staunchless love toward the lowliest
of His creatures.

Meditation upon the person for whom we would pray. Turning
our attention to human need, we seek to be consumed with loving

concern for the welfare of the one for whom we would pray. We join ourselves to him in his grief, pain, and need.

Lifting the person into God's presence. Now in prayer we take our friend into the fullness of the Presence where dwells the redemptive power. We "see" God at work. In our faith and love we realize that at this very moment he is at work for a good that exceeds our most enthusiastic expectations. Leslie D. Weatherhead's description of the prayers of intercession in City Temple, London, will clarify this and the previous step. Concerning an actual case, he writes: "Here is nurse so-and-so, a member of our church, a girl of nineteen, who is studying at such-and-such a hospital. She is suffering from such-and-such a disease. Her temperature is very high. She cannot sleep without drugs. She has not taken any food for some days. In imagination (I say to the people) go into the ward and stand with Christ next to her bed. Do not pray that she may become better, because that is putting her cure in the future. Believe that at this very moment Christ is touching her life, and that His healing power is being made manifest in her body now. Believe that He can more powerfully work in the atmosphere of our faith and love." After holding the praying congregation's attention to her for a few moments, he passes on to another person.

Closing the prayer. If the previous work has been well done, the needs and deficiencies of human experience will gradually fade before the sufficiency of God, and our loving concern will be illuminated by the knowledge of a greater love which has taken over. We may now briefly conclude our prayer by committing ourselves and the person for whom we pray into His care, thanking Him for His fatherly response, and putting the matter from our thoughts.

A second way of intercession which has issued in some striking results in group meditation follows these steps: Each person first selects three persons: a loved one, one toward whom he is indifferent, and an "enemy" who irritates him, in whose presence he feels uncomfortable, or toward whom he feels hostility.

Each person begins by praying for himself and continues in prayer until he senses God's love toward him and realizes that His Kingdom enfolds him. Each person then prays for his friend. It is easy to join the friend in the Kingdom of love, for we naturally want to include him. Next each one extends his prayer to include the indifferent or neutral person, the bus driver, store clerk, distant neighbor, or anyone else who has never been in his circle. God's love includes him also. In the Kingdom there is no separation and in the realm of the Spirit everyone is fully personal, never merely a thing. Imperceptibly he will become a part of the circle of love and faith.

Now it is possible to enfold the dark "enemy" as well. Beneath the forbidding exterior the "enemy" is seen as a struggling and striving human being. He, too, is a pilgrim, traveling toward God. God loves him as much as He loves the friend. Gradually the darkness gives way to the light, and the inclusiveness of the Kingdom becomes victorious over the separateness of hate. I have seen enmities of long standing melt into friendship, and gestures of kindness suddenly and unexpectedly made by the "enemy" thus prayed for.

A third way of intercession, described by Louise Eggleston of the World Literacy Prayer Group of Norfolk, Virginia, has certain similarities to the method used by Christian Scientists. In many cases it has proved to be successful after other ways of praying have not seemed to work. Unfortunately, it is a way of prayer that is easily misunderstood and may possibly be danger-ous if misapplied. The method has two phases: First, there is a prayerful analysis of the deepest spiritual needs of the person for whom help is sought. This phase is a prayer to the Holy Spirit for guidance and assumes that God knows the need best and is able and willing to direct the intercession when we are submissive to His leadings. Second, there is a channeling of positive suggestions to the person during sleep. These suggestions are spoken aloud, although not within the hearing of the sufferer. The person is addressed by name, as though he were listening. He is not told until long afterward, if at all, that he was prayed for in this way. He might misinterpret the origin of his new powers and so distrust them even before he can consolidate his new life.

The application of this way of prayer depends upon a willingness to look beyond symptoms to the deepest spiritual needs. The greatest temptation is that the method may be used to rid people of the outward evidences of trouble while neglecting their inward roots. The suggestions that are needed in most cases consist of assurances of being loved by God, of being capable of trusting Him, or of having some as yet unfulfilled purposes which God wishes to bless and further. The great spiritual truths reshaped for each particular case have authentic healing and recuperative power when shared in this way.

In conclusion, there are as many ways of intercession as there are people who pray. As the spirit and principles of this mode of prayer are progressively understood, intercession becomes a free improvisation in which one becomes a fit instrument for the enlarging circle of grace. As this occurs there dawns the realization that it is not we who pray, but God who prays through us.

CHAPTER 12

Problem-

Solving Prayer

The basis for problem-solving prayer is faith in God's ongoing creativity as unfolded in the foregoing chapters. Events have a nexus for completion. Existence seems to be a hierarchy of "wholes-under-construction" or wholes-coming-into-being. This is another way of saying that the Creator is perpetually at work for good in every situation. Through problem-solving prayer, we become in a literal sense "co-creators" with Him.

There are three ways of facing the problems of life: we may, literally or psychologically, run away. We may contest and fight our problems. Or we may follow the deep trend in events which is their "natural" course toward completion. The first two alternatives assume that the nature of existence is either hostile or at least neutral to our values. The last alternative rests on faith in God.

A story from the wisdom of an ancient Chinese sage, Chuang-tse, illustrates the way of co-operation with the tendencies in things:

"Prince Hui's cook was cutting up a bullock. Every blow of

his knife, every heave of his shoulders, every tread of his foot, every whssh of rent flesh, every chhk of the chopper, was in perfect harmony—rhythmical like the Dance of the Mulberry Grove, simultaneous like the chords of the Ching Shou.

" 'Well done!' cried the Prince. 'Yours is skill indeed.'

" 'Sire,' replied the cook, 'I have always devoted myself to Tao. It is better than skill. When I first began to cut up bullocks, I saw before me simply whole bullocks. After three years' practice I saw no more whole animals. And now I work with my mind and not with my eye. When my senses bid me stop, but my mind urges me on, I fall back upon eternal principles. I follow such openings or cavities as there may be, according to the natural constitution of the animal. I do not attempt to cut through joints, still less through large bones.

" 'A good cook changes his chopper once a year—because he cuts. An ordinary cook, once a month—because he hacks. But I have had this chopper nineteen years, and though I have cut up many thousands of bullocks, its edge is as if fresh from the whetstone. For at the joints there are always interstices, and the edge of a chopper, being without thickness, it remains only to insert that which is without thickness into such an interstice. By these means the interstice will be enlarged, and the blade will find plenty of room. It is thus that I have kept my chopper for nineteen years, as though fresh from the whetstone.

" 'Nevertheless, when I come upon a hard part, where the blade meets with a difficulty, I am all caution. I fix my eyes on it. I stay my hand, and gently apply the blade, until with a hwah the part yields like earth crumbling to the ground. Then I withdraw the blade and stand up and look around; and at last I wipe my chopper and put it carefully away.'

" 'Bravo!' cried the Prince. 'From the words of this cook I have learnt how to take care of my life.' "

The skill of this cook lies in the power to "see" or "hear"

M

trends and tendencies of existence when they are not clearly visible to the physical senses. "If you keep still and listen," writes Stewart Edward White, "things will always explain themselves. It is as if something drew near you, and formed, and revealed itself—something that holds itself at a distance when you don't listen."

The mystical kinship of all things in God suggests that when one investigates by letting questions arise from his own spiritual center and when he directs them to the center that is somehow hidden in the phenomena investigated, "things" seem to talk and yield their secret. George Washington Carver described his method of investigation into plants and their uses. He carried a flower into his laboratory and sat down humbly and appreciatively before it. Then he said, "Dear Creator, what did you make this flower for?" When he considered the peanut in this way, there flowed from the laboratory hundreds of commercially useful products which saved thousands of southern farmers from economic ruin. When rotation of crops appeared necessary to conserve the soil, he suggested sweet potatoes. Soon the cry went up that there was no market for the new crop. This time he entered the laboratory—"God's little workshop"—with a sweet potato. Again he found sufficient commercial uses for it to save a whole section of the country from impoverishment.

Another illustration from the ancient Chinese illuminates yet further the required attitudes and responses:

"Ch'ing the chief carpenter, was carving wood into a stand for musical instruments. When finished, the work appeared to those who saw it as though of supernatural execution; and the Prince of Lu asked him, saying, 'What mystery is there in your art?'

" 'No mystery, Your Highness,' replied Ch'ing. 'And yet there is something. When I am about to make such a stand, I guard against any diminution of my vital power. I first reduce my mind to absolute quiescence. Three days in this condition, and I become oblivious of any reward to be gained. Five days, and I become oblivious of any fame to be acquired. Seven days, and I become unconscious of my four limbs and my physical frame. Then, with no thought of the court present in my mind, my skill becomes concentrated, and all disturbing elements from without are gone. I enter some mountain forest, I search for a suitable tree. It contains the form required, which is afterwards elaborated. I see the stand in my mind's eye, and then set to work. Beyond that there is nothing. I bring my own native capacity into relation with that of the wood. What was suspected to be of supernatural execution in my work was due solely to this.' "

These illustrations should make it apparent that the whole-making tendency in events is not passive. Events are reshaped. They come out not jerry-built but Whole. As the writer of Ecclesiastes has said, "He has made everything beautiful in its time."

The Quaker meeting for business proceeds on this assumption. There is no voting. Every decision is unanimous. When differences develop, they are clarified, and then the meeting resolves into silence to seek divine help. Some new proposal is then made with the intent of including what was of worth in the conflicting points of view. So they proceed, alternating silence with discussion, until all are convinced. Much of the power of the Friends' witness derives from this trustful approach to human differences.

Two objections to this kind of prayer often arise: Should we not be more self-reliant rather than expecting God to solve problems which we ought to solve ourselves? Should we not simply adore God as an end in Himself rather than use Him to serve our own purposes?

The first objection must be answered by recurring to what we have written about the Incarnation and God's ongoing creativity in and through us. The question falsely presupposes a mechanical view of God's relationship to us and our relationship to Him.

God works in us as our very Self. When we allow Him to work, we discover that we are more completely at work than ever before. Thus problem-solving prayer is as much a process of coming alive to our own inner powers as it is a reliance on the resources of God. There is a sense in which these cannot be properly separated.

An answer to the second objection also depends upon what has been written earlier. In problem-solving we co-operate fully with God as He continually re-creates the world. Is not this a kind of adoration? Our orientation is toward His Kingdom, and our power is drawn from His strength. There is no room for the slightest degree of magical coercion of God to merely human ends. Properly understood, the whole business is to His glory.

SOME RULES OF PROBLEM-SOLVING PRAYER

Experience teaches that there are optimum conditions for this, as for other types of prayer. These conditions, or rules, if you will, are neglected only at the risk of disappointment and failure.

First of all, the problem must be stated as clearly as possible. It is even wise to ask pointed questions though without disposing oneself to a specific predetermined answer. We must give entire consent that the resolution be grounded in Truth and come from the Spirit of Wisdom, whom we invoke in prayer.

Furthermore, as in the prayer of petition, the problem must be an authentic and genuine concern. This earnestness may tempt us to prejudice the outcome, but we must resist this temptation. During the meditation we must maintain an attention at once alert and nonattached. The creative, inspiring Power must be permitted to work undeterred by our selfish itch to interfere and have things our way. The conducive attitude is that of relaxed trust and acceptance of whatever comes. We do not pass judgment or exclude elements which are offensive. They may all be part of the final solution.

Faith and expectancy must be joined to humility, which fosters an inner emptiness and defeats the false answers and inhibiting fears of the ego. In our moments of true humility we know that the total credit must be ascribed to the creator Spirit who works in and through us. In certain high moments our whole inner being will seem indistinguishable from this holy Power and His work. Through this intimate participation in the divine wisdom we may experience an ecstatic union reminiscent of that experienced by St. Paul, "I live, but not I, but Christ within me."

Throughout the work we must insulate ourselves against the dissipation of vital energies in petty distractions and irrelevancies by working with clear purpose and the total dedication of our full powers to the task. Only in this way can we prevent the meditation from turning into a daydream. But this purposiveness must not deny a sense of lift and joy to the undertaking. Joy is often the hallmark of the visitation of Spirit in creation.

A final rule is that illumination must be first tested and then acted upon. If the wisdom received is not taken seriously, then more will not be given. Unfortunately, Rufus Moseley speaks for most of us when he says, "I have never lacked guidance—only obedience."

A WAY OF PROBLEM-SOLVING PRAYER

Some years ago in *Living Religion,* Hornell Hart proposed a pattern of problem-solving prayer which, with some modification and addition, has proved exceedingly fruitful to me. It consists of seven steps.

Selection of the problem. This step may seem too elementary to note, but a little practice will show how essential it is. Unless the problem is carefully selected and adhered to wth stubborn purpose, the mind flits from one difficulty to another. Each will seem equally urgent and will usurp the place of its predecessor. An entire meditation may involve a clutter of problems no one of which will be attended to in any illuminating way.

Relaxation. We have to learn to give up trying, to realize when we are fairly beaten, and to surrender our own efforts into God's hands. At least for the duration of this meditation, we must realize that our work is to remain attentive but submissive, alert but passive. Our modern tenseness is so natural to us that we are inclined to interpret giving up as a sign of weakness and lack of self-respect. For this reason we will probably have to work paradoxically at not-working. Edmund Jacobson of the University of Chicago suggests a skilled approach to this which he calls "progressive relaxation." His principles, though developed for physical therapy, may be applied both to the body and to the psychic life of mind and emotion. (a) Letting go of the body. Sitting erect in a straight chair, we systematically release all tensions from the body. Such tensions are a form of distrust and a refusal to let the body alone to do its work without interference. This step may require a quarter of an hour through which we repeatedly move in imagination from head to toe and say to each set of muscles, "Let go!" Tensions in the face and neck will be the last to give up, but when they do we may go on to the next step, (b) letting go of feelings and emotions. We will be surprised how many of these will disappear along with the bodily tensions, but the rest must be surrendered completely. Every irritation, worry, or feeling of pleasure or joy must be handed over to God. We must keep nothing for ourselves.

We are now ready for the next phase, (c) letting go of our thoughts. Every idea is surrendered as it occurs. Now we claim nothing. We return to God the power of thought which He gave us. We take out the entire card index file of ideas and lay it upon the altar. All our learning, theories, and scientific concepts are to be made "captive to obey Christ." It may be necessary to reassure ourselves that God will give all these things back enriched and deepened. Our pride in "possessing" them and our mechanical way of manipulating them often make our knowledge a barrier instead of a gateway to wisdom.

The final phase in relaxation is (d) letting go of the will. All our plans and purposes, the best and the worst, are given to Him. Nothing must remain to us. God and His will must be everything.

Concentration. Having passed through the simplification of consciousness which occurs when relaxation has been attained, we now draw our attention to a focus. Since we are not yet dealing with our problem, the focus is for a moment like the clear light on the screen before a film is run. This is a period of quiet expectant waiting before the meditation actually begins.

Invocation. We remind ourselves of the Being in whose Presence this act of devotion is being carried forward. We may fleetingly call to mind the vast and unimaginable possibilities for good that are inherent in the wisdom and power of God. Here we call in faith and trust upon that power. This phase need not be long. Often a few seconds will suffice.

Meditation proper. We now bring into the steady, clear focus of the mind the problem which set us to praying. We may visualize or in some other way bring the elements of it before us. If the issue is one of personal relationships, we may see and hear the parties, including ourselves, in the characteristic situations. We look deeply and listen intently, expectantly waiting for some understanding which has eluded us. "You sit quietly and apart," writes Mary Austin of this type of prayer, "all the stray tags and streamers of your mind tucked in, all your energies folded and at hand. Then you run through your mind the problem which has inspired your need of prayer; you look it over intelligently, brushing aside gently all intrusive matter, not thrusting and clamping down on preferred aspects, but holding it easily with the flow of breath, falling away from it and coming back untiringly to the subjects of meditation."

Illumination. If we persist, understanding will begin to flow. An "opening" may suddenly appear, or perhaps some new and unexpected wisdom concerning the matter will appear to the mind. These things will occur in varying degrees, from a sense of peace and confidence toward the problem to a swift wordless grasp of the resolution.

Testing and application. It is wise to frame in words the clarification we have experienced. Now it must be applied, indeed, must be applied and practiced if more is to come. Obedience to such wisdom when it has been properly tested and evaluated is the surest pledge to our deepest selves that we really want wisdom, that we are willing to be channels of the divine Truth for the sake of that Truth alone.

When this way of problem-solving has been experienced a number of times, its principles can be employed in less formal ways. The purpose of special periods of meditation is to develop a habitual cast of mind which makes illumination second nature. Stewart Edward White describes this as an everyday practice. "Before I start anything," he writes, "I must drop my consciousness into place as a link between the Purpose I do not understand and the little act of which I am a master. It is the definite awareness of this hookup and the practice of it that makes it work, lets in the power. It's just a workaday natural action—my two hands directed by my spirit. If that were an accomplished habit, there would be no necessity for wrong or puzzlement. I would just say to the Unknown Purpose: 'I am ready when you are,' and keep a steady confidence in the purpose at hand; and in due course it would be accomplished better than I could plan it."

PRAYER FOR GUIDANCE

Prayer for guidance is based upon the same principles and follows the same general methods that have been examined in this and preceding chapters. It is based upon the assumption that there is a larger whole, unknown to us but known to God, into which our lives and actions properly fit. Guidance does not seek a full vision of that future; rather it seeks an illumination of the will in action so that what is decided and acted upon will contribute to that larger Whole. There is certainly an element of prevision in it. But it is largely a step-by-step affair. This is what Stewart Edward White calls a "pathfinding instinct." Julia de Beausobre speaks of it as "insight into the breadth of God's composition for this particular event on earth." And this is the proper way to think of guidance, for the future is not determined and depends to some degree upon our response to events and the extent of our creativity.

Sensitivity to guidance is similar to the homing instinct in animals and to the inexplicable behavior of insects. The evidence strongly suggests that some of their behavior is only understandable on the hypothesis of a whole of which the animal's body is only a part and to which the creature is able to respond in ways not traceable to the usual senses of sight, hearing, touch, or smell. There seems, furthermore, to be plausible mechanical account of the evolution of these patterns because the isolated elements of the pattern are useless for survival. Only the complete pattern would aid the organism's struggle for existence.

Karl Heim in *The Transformation of the Scientific World-View* gives a remarkable instance of the behavior of an insect, the *Sitaris* beetle, which seems to require an extrasensory explanation: This beetle "lays its eggs at the entrance of a subterranean passage made by a certain kind of bee (Anthophora). Why does it choose that precise point? Because the following events are 'clairvoyantly previsaged': The *Sitaris* larvae wait at the entrance to the passage until the male bee crawls out to make its nuptial flight. It [*sic*] climbs onto the bee's back and clings there during the flight of the bee. When, high in the air, the male bee has intercourse with the female bee, the larvae take this opportunity of changing planes in mid-air and move over to the female bee. When the female returns to the nest where she has built up her store of honey, she begins, after a time, to lay her eggs, and the *Sitaris* larva fastens upon an egg and destroys its interior in a few days. Then it uses the shell as a support and a raft so as not to sink into the honey, and floats on the surface of the honey, feeding on it until it is strong enough to develop into a fully fledged insect."

This is especially remarkable because the two organisms involved in the plan, the parent and the offspring, cannot communicate with each other. "And each action involved makes sense only on the assumption that all the rest will be successfully performed and the ultimate goal will be reached."

This account offers a suggestive analogy to the prayer for guidance. Something beyond the rational processes of observation and calculation is certainly involved in this life-cycle. Each phase of the insect's behavior is a response to a large whole which is in some dim manner felt and responded to. Man's life is analogous to this. Even in scientific studies we do not find the whole of which our actions are a part. Mystery shrouds God's purpose for our individual life as it does the larger meanings He is weaving in His providential governance of nations and races. Our faith in the prayer of guidance is that God will communicate His will if we tender our spirits to His intimations. He will not necessarily reveal the whole to the clear light of our understanding, but He will lead us, step by step and decision by decision, into a significant relationship to it.

Professor J. B. Rhine of Duke University has in his files many cases of long-distance homing of dogs and cats. In many of the cases no possible physical clues were available to the animal in his journey. Rhine assumes that the explanation must be extra-sensory. One typical instance is the story of Bosco, a handsome mongrel dog which belonged to the S. C. Flanigan family, of

Knoxville, Tennessee. "When Mrs. Flanigan closed her apartment and went to Glendale, California, she had Bosco crated and shipped to the coast. On arrival he was left at the express office over night. The following morning his crate was found empty. A large hole had been gnawed in the side. All searching for Bosco proved fruitless.

"On her return to Knoxville, Mrs. Flanigan moved to a new part of town and eight months elapsed before she visited her old neighborhood. A lean and bedraggled dog sat on the steps of her old apartment house. He greeted her joyously. A later check of color, spots, scars and other distinctive markings, as well as peculiar habits—including a way of walking due to an injury—adequately identified the dog as Bosco. Besides, Mrs. Flanigan and her three children knew him at once. A neighbor said that the animal had been sitting on the steps most of the time for two months."

Rhine concludes by asking, "How did he make the long journey home over thousands of miles of roads he never had seen before?" The explanation that seems to be required by the data is that there is a whole situation, larger than the one perceived through the senses, to which the animal is able to respond. Such an account, though only an analogue to human guidance, does illuminate it.

"Abraham went out not knowing whither he went," but he went under the guidance of God. He could not have determined what that tremendous future was to be. At his trial Socrates said that whenever he was in danger his "voice" always warned him, but on this day it had remained silent. He had faith that this lack of warning implied that the great adventure into death was for good, not for evil.

In the trying days of the Civil War, Abraham Lincoln said, "If it were not for my firm belief in an overruling Providence, it would be difficult for me, in the midst of such complications of affairs, to keep my reason on its seat." L. E. Chittenden, who was register of the treasury under Lincoln, gives in his *Recollections* these words of the President: "That the Almighty does make use of human agencies, and directly intervenes in human affairs, is one of the plainest statements of the Bible. I have had so many evidences of His direction, so many instances when I have been controlled by some other power than my own will, that I cannot doubt that this power comes from above. I frequently see my way clear to a decision when I am conscious that I have no sufficient facts upon which to found it. But I cannot recall an instance in which I have followed my own judgment, founded upon such a decision, where the results were unsatisfactory; whereas, in almost every instance where I have yielded to the views of others, I have had occasion to regret it." Lincoln's conclusion on this matter states the fundamental faith which undergirds all prayer for guidance: "I am satisfied that when the Almighty wants me to do or not to do a particular thing, he finds a way of letting me know it."

To one learning to tender his spirit to the intimations of God's guiding Spirit a word of advice is needed. All guidance, from whatever source, needs checks. "Welcome your hunch," advises Stewart Edward White, "and examine it!" In this he echoes the words of St. John, "Try the spirits whether they are of God." Checking does not mean to demand proof. The future cannot be proved in advance. Nevertheless, authentic answers to prayers of problem solving and guidance can stand up to three tests: The tests elicited from one's own conscience, the test of comparison with the enlightened judgment of the community of those who are faithfully seeking to live under the guidance of the Spirit, and, lastly, the test of comparison with the traditions of Christian wisdom in Scripture and history. The Spirit whose wisdom we seek has enlightened others, and He has revealed Himself as the Christ in Jesus of Nazareth. He speaks with the same voice to all who seek Him with a whole heart.

As one becomes seasoned in seeking God's guidance for the particular problems and events of life, the whole begins to knit together into a coherent unity. There dawns the wonder of an over-all life direction or vocation—in the literal sense of the word, a "calling." Through all the special leadings there gradually emerges a master direction, an orientation which controls the whole of life, not abstractly as a principle, but concretely as a Way in which to walk. This leads us on from petition to the rest of the life of prayer, and especially to joyful thanksgiving and deeper commitment.

CHAPTER 13

Commitment

and Thanksgiving

No prayer is complete without an act of self-offering. "God does not ask of us either sensible devotion," writes John Nicholas Grou, "or those great lights on which self-love feeds but too much." God does not ask that we be proficient masters of the arts of prayer. Pride and self-will may taint all of these. "What God asks of us, above all things," Abbe Grou tells us again, "is the entire resignation and abandonment of ourselves to Him—a resignation of all without exception and for ever." In such commitment alone can we avoid the blasphemy of using God as a means to self-realization, and become instead the means of glorifying Him.

The spirit which should infuse all prayer, whether of adoration, confession, or petition, is expressed in the words of the Liturgy of the Holy Communion: "Here we offer and present unto Thee, O Lord, ourselves, our souls and bodies, to be a reasonable, holy, and living sacrifice unto Thee."

This is a law of prayer: God can give only to the degree that we give ourselves to Him. The way of receiving is through giving. But it must be remembered that this giving, this commitment, must be totally for the glory of God and without the slightest thought of receiving. For commitment comes when we see that in the light of the love that overflows from God, no other response will do. Then we learn, often long afterward, that He has returned our meager self-offering a thousandfold. This has marked the prayers of the saints. Bishop Westcott reminds us: "The mark of a saint is not perfection but consecration. A saint is not a man without faults, but a man who has given himself without reserve to God."

Commitment is both general and specific. We offer ourselves to the awesome Goodness, desiring that we may be to Him "as a man's hand is to a man." Then, as in Isaiah's case, we hear the commissioning voice directing us to the tasks which He has for our time. At this point the spiritual life turns to details. We are compelled to be a certain type of person with specific beliefs and engaged in specific acts. This demand offends the spiritual promiscuity of an age which offers endless hospitality to ideas and deliberations pro and con. Here we are faced with the either-or of choice and responsibility. "My listeners," Kierkegaard asked, "do you at present live in such a way that you are yourself clearly eternally conscious of being an individual?" Our reply is often that of Willy Loman in *The Death of a Salesman*, "I still feel temporary about myself."

Dante in his description of Hell recounts a moment just inside the dreadful gate where he was greeted with "sighs, with lamentations and loud moans," by a band who his guide Virgil explains are "those who had passed their time (for living it could not be called) in a state of apathy and indifference to the good and evil." Some of these were fallen angels who had proved neither rebellious nor true to God, "but for themselves were only."

One of the great evils of our time is the vagueness and emptiness of the inner life of most people. They all strive to be alike, to be liked, to offend no one. Observing, appreciating, and reflecting are not a sufficient medicine for this evil. Only complete and unreserved commitment to the will of God can break the hypnotic power of social approval and disapproval and lead on to authentic personhood and individuality. Total commitment, not in one heroic gesture, but in every time of prayer, is that daily dying to self which puts an end to the duality at the center of our being and leads to that purity of heart and singleness of eye which our Lord assures us will bring a vision of God.

THANKSGIVING

The great rhythm of the Church's liturgical life is one of praise and thanksgiving. That is, it is Eucharistic. The total self-offering of Christ, and the self-giving of God in and through that accepted offering, are the food of eternal life for all. Such is the mystery of the Holy Communion. In celebrating this mystery we offer not only ourselves, but also "our sacrifice of praise and thanksgiving." This is simple Christian realism, an acknowledgment of our boundless obligation to the love revealed to us in Christ.

> It is a joy to give thanks to the Eternal,
>   to sing thy praise, O thou Most High,
> to proclaim thy goodness in the morning
>   and thy faithfulness at night.

The fully awakened God consciousness cannot help singing in gratitude. The joy of the psalmist is echoed by St. Francis in his celebrated "Canticle of the Sun":

> O most high, almighty, good Lord God, to Thee belong praise, glory, honor, and all blessings!
> Praised be my Lord God with all His creatures; and especially

KING PENGUIN
KING PENGUIN
KING PENGUIN
KING PENGUIN
KING PENGUIN

**A
major new
paperback
series
bringing you
the best modern
literature
from all corners
of the globe.**

KING PENGUIN
KING PENGUIN
KING PENGUIN
KING PENGUIN
KING PENGUIN
KING PENGUIN
KING PENGUIN
KING PENGUIN

1981

KING PENGUINS

May
A CONFEDERACY OF DUNCES
John Kennedy Toole
LABYRINTHS
Jorge Luis Borges
LAMB
Bernard Mac Laverty
THE ORCHID TRILOGY
Jocelyn Brooke
THE VIRGIN IN THE GARDEN
A. S. Byatt
THE YAWNING HEIGHTS
Alexander Zinoviev

June
THE BLOODY CHAMBER AND
OTHER STORIES
HEROES AND VILLAINS
Angela Carter

July
SOLARIS/CHAIN OF CHANCE/
PERFECT VACUUM
Stanislaw Lem
VOSS
Patrick White

August
BLACK TICKETS
Jayne Anne Phillips
TITUS ALONE
Mervyn Peake

September
FIRE ON THE MOUNTAIN
Anita Desai
THE LOVE DEPARTMENT
William Trevor

October
WINTER DOVES
David Cook
THE BEGGAR MAID
Alice Munro

November
THE TWYBORN AFFAIR
Patrick White
THE HEART IS A LONELY HUNTER
Carson McCullers

December
THE TRANSIT OF VENUS
Shirley Hazzard
TITUS GROAN
Mervyn Peake

9088

our brother the sun, who brings us the day, and who brings us the light . . .

Praised be my Lord for our sister the moon, and for the stars, the which He has set clear and lovely in heaven.

Praised be my Lord for our brother the wind, and for air and cloud, calms and all weather, by the which Thou upholdest in life all creatures.

Praised be my Lord for our sister water, who is very serviceable unto us, and humble, and precious, and clean.

Praised be my Lord for our brother fire, through whom Thou givest us light in the darkness. . . .

Praised be my Lord for our mother the earth, the which doth sustain us and keep us, and bringeth forth divers fruits, and flowers of many colors, and grass.

Praised be my Lord for all those who pardon one another for His love's sake, and who endure weakness and tribulation. . . .

Praised be my Lord for our sister, the death of the body. . . .

Praise ye, and bless ye the Lord, and give thanks unto Him, and serve Him with great humility.

Such a spirit of thanksgiving is another of the great rules of prayer. Engaged by a whole heart, it wipes away all discouragement and lack of faith. It helps us to realize that God works in the present and not merely in the probable future. In his Gospel, St. John reports that at the tomb of Lazarus, Jesus, *before* calling his friend from death, raised his voice and cried, "Father, I thank thee that thou hast heard me." Thanksgiving is in this way an affirmation of the present power of God toward us that dissolves our doubts and lifts our hopes.

There are dangers in thanksgiving. A man may insincerely participate in the forms of thanks without having the inner spirit of the thankfulness. On the other hand, when enumerating God's gifts, he may imagine that he is especially privileged and one of the Lord's favorites. But these dangers are far less threatening than those which stem from prayer that is devoid of the spirit

N

of gratitude and praise. As one learns to thank God for His greatest and most universal gifts, these dangers disappear altogether.

We should thank God for His grace which abounds in the natural order to all men; for the beauty of color, rhythm and form; for the saints whose winsomeness makes faith a joy, reminding us, as St. Francis says, of the sweetness of God; for Christ, his life, death, and resurrection; for the creative work of the Spirit in works of love and prayer; and even for prayer itself.

> I love to know that the
>   Eternal listens
> to the voice of my appeal;
> because he bends his ear to me,
> I will pray to him all my life.

Heartfelt commitment and thanksgiving express that total acknowledgment of God which we have described in the prayer of adoration, that outpouring of gifts of love which we have come to know in confession and petition in all their forms, and that joy which enraptures us in the moment of communion. When we come to know the Eternal in these ways, we join the chorus of those that fall before the throne and cry, "Worthy art thou, our Lord and our God, to receive glory and honor and power."

CHAPTER 14

Finding Reality

Through Meditation

Mental prayer is the classical name for the systematic use of imagination, will, feeling, and reason in meditation. It is a highly disciplined and conscious form of prayer. In the period following the Reformation, Roman Catholics gave special attention to the development of mental prayer. Except among certain mystical sects, like the Society of Friends, Protestants have neglected it, although in a sense the long sermon and the devotional reading of the Scriptures performed some of the same functions for Protestant devotion. Non-Roman Catholics ought to renew their cultivation of so powerful and useful a form of prayer.

Ministers and laymen become enthusiastic for this "new" instrument when they are guided to an understanding of it. Even children gladly follow those directed meditations which they are capable of envisaging.

A WAY OF MENTAL PRAYER—THE SULPICIAN METHOD

One of the most widespread forms of mental prayer, known as the Suplician Method, is a consolidation and simplification of

many earlier methods. Its underlying concepts have come to us
from the work of St. Jean Eudes and the French clerics Cardinal
Berulle, Father de Condren, and Father Olier. Back of them,
however, lie other classical methods, specifically: (1) the method
of Ignatius Loyola which puts great emphasis upon imagination
(summoning the aid of all the senses in meditation) and will
power; (2) the Franciscan methods, which are, according to
Bede Frost, "distinctly affective in character," and follow the devotional life of St. Francis of Assisi; and (3) the Dominican
methods which emphasize objective theological content, praise,
and adoration.

The method of St. Sulpice by combining all these features
offers the possibility of wide use in modern devotional life. In
the *Art of Mental Prayer,* Bede Frost points out that this type of
prayer invariably has three parts: preparation, meditation proper,
and conclusion. The preparation should begin long before the
meditation hour itself. Father Adolphe Tanquerey in *The Spiritual Life,* a Suplician text, says that the person who would become
proficient must practice as far as possible a habitual mortification
of the senses and passions, humility, and a continuous recollection
(recalling the mind to an awareness of God). Assuming this
"remote preparation," as it is called, the subject of meditation is
selected the night preceding and is made the last thought upon
going to sleep. Upon rising, it is brought to mind again.

When we prepare to meditate, we consciously place ourselves
in the presence of God whom we know to be present everywhere
and especially in the heart. We humble ourselves before Him because of our sins, and, by an act of true contrition and penitence,
we join ourselves in faith to Christ. Furthermore, acknowledging
that we are incapable of praying as we ought, we invite the Holy
Spirit to pray through us.

The meditation itself has three steps: Jesus before the eyes,
Jesus in the heart, and Jesus in the hands. In the first step we

are an alert and devout observer. We consider every aspect of the subject of meditation. The whole scene is reconstructed by the use of all the senses. We bring to mind the touch, taste, smell, feel, and look of everything. In a Biblical scene, for example, the heat of the sun may be felt, the dust tasted, and the fresh fall of rain smelled. The color of the hills and lake, the shape of the buildings, the look of people must come before the mind in as rich and complete a manner as may be possible. Because most of our conscious life is filled with such sense images, an over-powering realism is lent to meditation through them. As we watch the scene unfold before us, we offer the homage of admiration, adoration, praise, thanksgiving, and love.

In the second step—Jesus in the heart—we join the scene as a participant. In the healing of the palsied man, for example, we see ourselves lowered through the roof on a stretcher and into the presence of Jesus. Hearing his words of healing—"Son, thy sins are forgiven!"—we react inwardly as though they had been spoken directly to us, and we feel the flow of full physical strength at the command, "Rise and walk!" This active role enables us to live through a spiritual encounter and respond to it as though the Lord were physically present to our senses.

The final step—Jesus in the hands—concerns the quality of our will. We ask, what must I do in the light of what I have seen and experienced? Repentance, resolutions, and plans are followed by a season of prayer for the grace to carry them out.

The conclusion consists of thanks to God for the graces given in meditation, request for His blessing on our resolutions, and the selection of some striking thought or maxim that impressed us during the meditation and that we use throughout the day as a means of remembrance.

The Sulpician Method applies to material which can be apprehended through the senses. By a slight alteration, the same technique can be useful in meditation upon abstract principle, nonpictorial passages of Scripture, or doctrines of faith. The preparation and conclusion remain substantially the same, but the body of the meditation follows this pattern: What does the subject before the intellect mean? What does the subject before the feelings mean to me? What must I do about the subject before the will?

An actual meditation on the theme "Who am I?" might proceed as follows: *Realization of what I am not.* I am not my body, but that which uses my body. I am not my emotions or my thoughts, but that which feels and thinks them. I am not my past, nor my brain and nervous system, nor any of my ego apparatus; these are all instruments through which the Self expresses itself. I am not my instincts, reflexes, drives, and appetites, nor am I the collections of socio-cultural egos which the demands and expectations of society cultivate in me. Yet all these things have an intimate though strange relationship to me and a profound bearing upon who I am.

Realization of what I am. I am embodied spirit among other embodied spirits in the midst of Spirit. I am created in the image of the Eternal Spirit. I am embodied will to live and a mysterious center of striving and growth. "I am will to live in the midst of life which wills to live." Yet I am unique and unlike any other being in the universe. Essentially I am boundless in that no limit can be set on my thought or feeling. Yet I am a creature and not the author of my own being. I am confronted by the absolute claim of a Holy and Perfect Being. By this confrontation I am bound in unlimited love and obligation to God and my fellow human beings.

I am not yet what I am to be, for I am in the process of becoming what I really am. My real Self is an ideal possibility of what I truly am in the purposes of God who created me and intends to re-create me in His image, who presses upon me and offers to be formed in me as the living Christ. He is my real center and my authentic Self. Apart from Him I am nothing.

Realization of what I am to do. What does this realization of my true being mean to me? How can I ever view myself in the same old conventional ways again? How can I ever fear or dissemble? I must cease being led captive to illusory notions of myself and my fellows, alter my meaningless pattern of living, and make room for God's purposes. I intend to do this . . . and this . . . and this! God help me. Christ help me. Amen.

A good plan in the use of a theme is to arrange the material so that it begins on the simplest levels and then progressively enlarges in scope and significance until it joins with the whole Spiritual world. Some themes that are especially suited to this type of meditation are love, life, time, or a profound theme of theology. The prayer should not be considered as an exercise in rational thinking. To be sure, we will marshal our best thoughts, but the purpose is to "realize" these truths inwardly and to "see through" their profoundest spiritual significance. Moreover, our purpose is to unite the very substance of our selves to our meditation and to incarnate its truth in feeling, thought, and action.

I can in imagination see Albert Schweitzer seated in the stern of a boat that inches slowly up the steaming Ogowe river. With poised alertness, he glances at the African jungle and its teeming abundance of animal life. He reflects on the will to live that is so vividly exhibited before his eyes. For months the same reflections have returned to his mind at moments such as these. The quiet brooding continues during the tedious hours. At last there dawns upon his consciousness the phrase which has become the text of both his life and thought—"Reverence for life." Such meditation is more than philosophic ratiocination; it is a form of communion with existence. In that profound dialogue of spirit, man reaches out, and Reality responds with a gift of life and wisdom.

The man who wishes to know the fullness of this method of mental prayer will keep a notebook of themes which may be drawn from the Bible, classics of devotion, great biographies, even science and literature. The themes should always be developed in such a way that, intersecting at several points our own experience, they challenge and transform us. Gerald Heard wisely suggests a thirty-day cycle of meditations. In this way we return at least once a month to the same themes, but not so often that they lose their freshness.

A profoundly moving series of meditations for Lent, for example, could be forty scenes and sayings from the life of our Lord. During the summer, meditation might be direct to the theme of a "Faith for the Whole of My Life." All our basic assumptions and experiences can be woven into a new and more true reflection of Christian wisdom. The Christian Year will provide a good guide in which unity and variety may be combined in a yet larger cycle of meditations. We must not rely too heavily on outside suggestions or substitute reading for meditation. The body of the meditation should be a free improvisation in which the Spirit of God is the prime mover. Finally, such prayers should always close with self-examination, resolution, and commitment.

Turning from the type of mental prayer suggested by the Sulpician Method, we may note quite a different type of mental prayer. Evelyn Underhill describes it in her *Practical Mysticism*. Its objective is an elementary contemplation that seeks to pass beyond discursive reasoning and conscious imagining to illumination. The pattern is as follows: Select some object such as a pencil. Then, develop discursive reflections concerning it: its origin, its relationship to society, its relationship to the universe, and so on. Thought may range widely, but must always return to the object in view. After a while conscious thought processes will begin to slow down and almost stop. The object will now begin to "speak to you." It will begin to yield unsuspected meaning, beauty, and power. "A perpetual growth of significance keeps pace with the increase of attention which you bring to bear on it." If this concentrated focus is maintained there comes a moment when "you sink as it were into the deeps of it, rest in it, 'unite' with it."

In *A Life of One's Own*, Joanna Field describes an experience with this type of meditation. The object of her meditation was a small tin mug. In spite of its ugliness she kept her attention focused on it for fifteen minutes. She writes: "I simply let its form imprint itself upon my mind. Slowly I became aware of a new knowledge. I seemed to sense what I can only call the 'physics' of the mug. Instead of merely seeing its shape and color I felt what I described to myself as its 'stresses and strains,' the pressures of its roundness and solidity and the table holding it up. This sense did not come at once and I suppose might never have come if I had not sat still and waited."

She found that listening to music in this way led her into an entirely new world, into the beauty of

> music heard so deeply
> That it is not heard at all, but you are the music
> While the music lasts.

She noted that there were resistances. Not only was there the constant temptation to let the mind follow after distractions which interrupted the meditation; there was also a certain resistance to surrendering, a panic of being lost, of being terribly hurt. Quite by accident she learned that this is the only way in which visual art yields up its secret. Delight and vision came only when she stopped trying. Looking at a Cézanne still-life, she became too tired to try to like or understand it. Her mind stopped meddling, and the invisible feelers of consciousness reached out, surrounded, and lived in what was being perceived. She simply gazed passively though alertly at the painting. Then the new dimensions began to unfold.

SOME RESULTS OF MENTAL PRAYER

In the skilled practice of mental prayer we control our lives through spiritual reconditioning. Imagination and thought are divine gifts which make possible our freedom from the arbitrary social conditioning which has made us what we are. Recorded on our nervous system and in our subconscious are all the impressions received throughout our lives. Together they largely dominate our attitudes and behavior. Through mental prayer, by taking command of this conditioning process and feeding the mind a judiciously selected diet of concepts, values, and attitudes, we can largely determine the person we are to become.

The principles of this form of prayer have been employed in Chinese so-called "brainwashing." The "students" are required to fill their minds with theories and facts which have only one general significance. They are given problems to work out in terms of these doctrines. If they do well, they are rewarded; and if not, they are punished. By keeping them in a state of chronic hunger, food becomes their most powerful reward, and withholding it a most severe punishment. In this way motivation to "learn" the lesson is greatly increased. This procedure is carried out in isolation from any possible intrusion of conflicting ideas or distractions. The "students" never see people nor read reports which might conflict with what they are supposed to learn. Furthermore, to remove the inevitable countersuggestions that would come between lessons from critical conversations among the men, the inner structure of the group is eroded by a system of informers. Anyone carrying negative reports of his fellows is rewarded, but the victims of the report are not punished. In this way informing subsequently appears as a harmless way to increase one's comforts, and nearly all become informers. The net effect of this policy is to make everyone in the camp so suspicious of his neighbor that serious conversation practically ceases. In such an environment the "student" gradually succumbs to the one-pointed suggestions; new emotions, convictions, and concepts take the place of the old. When this is continued long enough, only the most hardy fail to succumb.

The exceptions would be those who had trained themselves in mental prayer. Julia de Beausobre, a citizen of the Russian Ukraine whose husband had been identified as a center of discontent, was arrested and incarcerated in the dread Lubianka prison. For six terrible months she was subjected to the processes by which her captors hoped to make the doors of her mind swing open and reveal all the persons who had ever come to her home or contacted her husband, however innocently. She knew she must keep these names from pouring out in her semidelirious moments as well as in the moments of conscious resistance to the torture. Her defense had to be deep within the mind itself. She could not risk even thinking of her previous political life. Every day she spent many hours picturing scenes of her childhood: sunsets, wooded walks, winter snow scenes, the night sky spread with blazing stars. When her torturers reduced her to semiconsciousness through physical torture, fatigue, and incessant questioning, her tongue simply babbled about all of these natural beauties. But she offered neither words of incriminating evidence nor the names of friends.

This is not possible, however, merely as a trick. The mind which is to undertake such a discipline must be free and unrepressed. Only a long training in the prayer of purgation and confession, which peels off the layers of unreality in the soul and lays bare the image of God that was originally there, can prepare one for such an ordeal. Mme. Beausobre has said, "When under torture, the layers of the self are stripped off, the divine image shines all the more brightly." Instead of madness, which was the usual result of such prolonged isolation and torment, she found Reality more clear than ever before.

This is impossible to a person without faith. The man who believes that only in the human brain do purpose, consciousness, and truth live, will discover no sure rock upon which to rest his being when his own poor brain is being filled with fantasies and madness by a fiendish and systematic method. Phillipe Vernier, the French pacifist, was sane and joyous after two years in solitary confinement. Normally a fraction of that time turns the hardiest into madmen. Because the content of their minds has all been determined by society and the accidents of life history, they have no further resource when the social support of their being is withdrawn. For the saint, however, when men are absent or prove totally hostile, God still remains, and He is more than sufficient.

This suggests a second result of mental prayer. A coherent unified person emerges from what had previously been a dumping ground of incongruous thoughts and experiences. This occurs as we come progressively to a profound realization of the truth of the spiritual life. This realization is more than intellectual assent; rather it is the assent of the whole being and all its powers. A luminous passage from the pen of James Martineau describes this act of realization: "Let any true man go into silence: strip himself of all pretense, and selfishness, and sensuality, and sluggishness of soul; lift off thought after thought, passion after passion, till he reaches the inmost depth of all; remember how short a time and he was not at all; how short a time again, and he will not be here; open his window and look upon the night, how still its breath, how solemn its march, how deep its perspective, how ancient its forms of light; and think how little he knows except the perpetuity of God, and the mysteriousness of life;— and it will be strange if he does not feel the Eternal Presence as close upon his soul as the breeze upon his brow; if he does not say, 'O Lord, art thou ever near as this, and have I not known thee?' "

THE PROBLEM OF DISTRACTIONS

Everyone who has ever undertaken to master the art of mental prayer has been plagued by distractions. Most people do not realize how chaotic their mental processes are until they attempt some of the exercises outlined above. The distractions that beset our meditations do not stem from the same source. Many of them spring from our passional nature and from the multitude of unconverted, hidden cross-purposes of our life. When we retire to meditate, Evelyn Underhill reminds us, "we cannot merely shut the door at the top of the basement stairs and hope for the best." The unsanctified remainder of life raises a wild disturbance. In the *House of the Soul,* she warns: "The loud voices of unmortified nature, saying, 'I want! I will! I won't! rising up from the kitchen premises, will ruin the delicate music of the upstairs wireless. Here is the source of all the worst distractions in prayer, and the lair of the devils that tempt us most: our inclinations to selfish choices, inordinate enjoyments, claimful affection, self-centered worry, instinctive avoidance of sacrifice and pain—all the downward drag of animal life."

But some distractions, as Aldous Huxley has observed, do not rise from the passions. Of many distractions, he says, "Their essence is to be irrelevant and pointless." In our moments of attempted recollection there will come to surface, along with the passional material, "a bobbing scum of miscellaneous memories, notions and imaginings—childhood recollections of one's grandmother's Skye terrier, the French name for henbane, a white-knightish scheme for catching incendiary bombs in mid-air—in a word, every kind of nonsense and silliness." We have two enemies here, the unmortified passions—the maniac in us—and the perennial propensity to distraction—the imbecile. Huxley is plainly correct: "The imbecile in us is as radically God's enemy as the passionate and purposeful maniac, with his insane cravings and aversions."

The struggle with distractions demands a twofold strategy: one, skill in the time of prayer itself, the other a larger campaign of discipline which gradually subdues behavior and thought to

spiritual ends. Of the latter, much has been said already. Of the
former, we can do no better than take advice which comes from
the teachers of interior prayer who tell us that although we
should be diligent and watchful in recalling our wandering
thoughts, a direct contest with them is futile. The very fact
that we attend to them gives them power over us. *The Cloud of
Unknowing* advices that "if any new thought or stirring of sin"
comes between us and God, "try to look as it were over their
shoulders, seeking another thing, the which is God." In *The
Guide to True Peace*, another anonymous author suggests that
"by calling to mind that we are in the Divine Presence, and endeavouring to sink down under a sense and perception thereof,
simply turning inwards, we wage insensibly a very advantageous,
though indirect war with them."

In this highly disciplined and conscious type of prayer we need
constantly to remind ourselves that God is the inspirer of our
most original, good, and fruitful thoughts. Nothing will destroy
so quickly all our best efforts as the illusion that we are the prime
mover in mental prayer. We may call meditation a pathway to
Reality, but it would be more correct to call it the opening
through which Reality reaches us. When the Divine Other begins
to infuse our considerations with His Presence, we have passed
beyond mental prayer to the communion for which it was the
intended means.

CHAPTER 15

The Life

of Communion

There comes a moment in high prayer which can best
be called a moment of communion. Dylan Thomas describes
such elevated absorption in "Vision and Prayer":

> I turn the corner of prayer and burn
> In a blessing of the sudden Sun.
> In the name of the damned
> I would turn back and run
> To the hidden land
> But the loud Sun
> Christens down
> The sky.
> I
> Am found.
> O let him
> Scald me and wound
> Me in his world's wound.
> His lightning answer my
> Cry. My voice burns in his hand.
> Now. I am lost in the blinding
> One. The sun roars at the prayer's end.

All Christian prayer verges toward such communion. The awesome Beauty which moves through every mood of devotion gradually and irresistibly attracts toward Himself alone. Adoration of the transcendent Being, the *"Mysterium Tremendum,"* who is always and forever beyond us, gradually yields to an intimate friendship. "It is a characteristic token of the difference between the two covenants," remarks Bishop Lightfoot, "that under the Law the 'fear of the Lord' holds very much the same place as 'faith in God,' 'faith in Christ,' under the Gospel. Awe is the prominent idea in the earlier dispensation, trust in the later." Through faith in the God who is the Father of Our Lord Jesus Christ, we know that we are friends and sons, and no longer servants. The great God has come across the abyss which separates Him from us, and we are invited into the intimate fellowship of a life "hid with Christ in God."

A similar transformation is to be found in other modes of prayer. *Confession* rises through the mists of egocentricity to a Reality-orientation which is a constant intercourse with the divine Life in the most common problems of existence. *Petition,* stimulated by earthy need, climaxes in an act of complete renunciation, a total submission to the divine Will in and for itself. *Intercession* begins and ends in communion with the loving Father who first rouses pity in us, and then inflames our faith so that together we and those for whom we pray rise into His healing Presence. *Mental prayer* begins as a conscious exercise, but, as one by one the barriers drop, the object of our meditation becomes a luminous intermediary through which the awesome Light shines.

Thus all prayer, no matter how mundane its subject matter, is enclosed in a climate of communion, but when communion becomes the exclusive preoccupation of prayer, mysticism emerges.

Mysticism is the disciplined glance which perceives a divine light shining through the most opaque substances, the belief that everything, being what it is, is symbolic of something more. It is, as Dean Ralph Inge once wrote, "the attempt to realize, in thought and feeling, the immanence of the temporal in the eternal, and of the eternal in the temporal."

Like mental prayer, the practice of mystical prayer is a familiar subject in Roman Catholic theology, and the late Richard Roberts of the United Church of Canada suggests that "we shall do well to extract from it what will enable us to practice 'interior prayer' with an evangelical simplicity."

Mystical theology teaches a threefold way to God: the purgative way, the illuminative way, and the unitive way. The first way is a period of reorientation and reshaping of life habits in preparation for the pilgrimage to God. It consists of severe disciplines and the heroic practice of the virtues. The second way is a season of visions, inspirations, and encounters in which the soul is lead, step by step, to the light of God. Visions, raptures, and illuminations cease at the third and highest level, and, at last, in the unitive way, the barriers fall as man is "oned" with God.

There are two major traditions of mystical devotion. The first, which I will call world-denying mysticism, seeks to find God by progressively turning away from the creation to the Creator, or, as Dean Inge phrases it, to "gain infinity by reducing self and the world to zero." A great spiritual director, Augustine Baker, grounds "the necessity of abstraction" in this: "The Divine union in spirit cannot be attained without an exclusion of all other inferior strange images and affections; therefore, by the means of abstraction, the soul is obliged to bring herself to as much unity, vacancy, and simplicity as may be." And Dionysius the Areopagite, father of negative theology in the West, says the mystic "must leave behind all things both in the sensible and in the intelligible worlds, till he enters into the darkness of nescience [not knowing] that is truly mystical."

There is a difference of opinion among theologians and historians as to whether this is an authentic development of impulses within Christian piety or whether it is an import from Asian sources. Dean Inge regards "the *via negativa* in metaphysics, religion, and ethics as the great accident of Christian Mysticism." But accident or not, it perfumes the writings of mystics whether Protestant or Roman Catholic. Even Tauler, one of the greatest of their number, though he avers that "Christ never arrived at the emptiness of which these men talk," repeats the negative formulas for pages together.

The second tradition, which I will call world-affirming mysticism, is reflected in the *Logos* doctrine of the Gospel of St. John which finds the Eternal involved in the normal course of nature and the divine Word in the normal process of human thought and feeling. Its roots are in the Hebraic refusal to see anything about the creation, save sin, which must be rejected or transcended in order to find God. "How foolish and hopeless," declares Martin Buber, "would be the man who turned aside from the course of his life in order to see God; even though he won all the wisdom and solitude and all the power of concentrated being he would miss God." Other roots of the world-affirming mysticism are in the Neo-Platonic tradition which, as interpreted by Augustine, seeks the divine not at the bottom of the scale of being in the formless "Infinite" but at the top in the fullness. "What is this which flashes upon me," cries Augustine, "and thrills my heart without wounding it? I tremble and I burn; I tremble, feeling that I am unlike Him; I burn, feeling that I am like Him."

Yet another important source of this form of piety lies in the life-affirming ethical perspectives of the Judeo-Christian tradition. Following in this tradition the philosopher Immanuel Kant insisted upon the irreducible reality of moral experience. And in our own day, Albert Schweitzer teaches that the path to union with God lies through the deepening of the ethical impulses until man comes to a universal "reverence for life." Such moral realism has affected nearly all the mystics in the Christian West. Even that ardent devotee of world-renouncing piety, Meister Eckhardt, in his *Talks of Instruction,* preached: "As I have often said, if a person were in such a rapturous state as St. Paul once entered, and he knew of a sick man who wanted a cup of soup, it would be far better to withdraw from the rapture for love's sake and serve him who is in need."

Disentangling these two traditions, interwoven as they are in the same personalities and bodies of religious instruction, is admittedly precarious. Dionysius says in one place, "all distinctions are lost in the absolute," and yet elsewhere he affirms the Christian qualities of deity with the fine words, "Divine Love is an eternal circle, from goodness, through goodness, and to goodness." The hazards of this two-type analysis, however weighty its scholarly precedents, must be acknowledged. But what is important is not the theological distinction but its fruits: two distinct types of prayer discipline and two decisively different consequences to the practitioners of those disciplines.

The praxis of abstractive mysticism is a process of extreme simplification, the removal of all creaturely and finite things. This rule demands first a rearrangement of the outward life toward voluntary poverty, celibacy, and the renunciation of social authority and position. It requires the reduction both of activity and the occasions of sense experience. Unnecessary social contacts, even with friends, must be ruthlessly curtailed. "Going out were never so good," says the *Theologia Germanica,* "but staying at home were better." During periods of contemplation the physical simplification is carried further by an extreme quieting of the body in a remote and undisturbed place. Even breathing is sometimes controlled to induce yet more profound bodily stillness.

The outer simplification is paralleled by an inner: the progressive banishment of sensory symbols, reflections, feelings, and even resolutions. Miguel de Molinos, a seventeenth-century Catholic quietist, taught the formula: silence of the mouth; silence of the mind; silence of the will.

World-denying mysticism finds no place for adoration, confession, and petition as they have been described in these pages. For according to the abstractive method, to pray about the world, its events, and persons, even on behalf of the highest values, merely binds the soul to illusion and loses the One in multiplicity.

Certain difficulties with the praxis of negative mysticism make it, in my opinion, unsuitable for wide contemporary use. At the outset we are confronted with the denial of values which have come to us through the natural life. To be sure, in the modern cultural collapse, these values have been so perverted that there is a strong temptation, in moments of weariness, to forsake them and the world of which they are a part. But the poet W. B. Yeats expresses our more virile convictions: "How can we who have read so much poetry, seen so many paintings, listened to so much music, where the cry of the flesh and the cry of the soul seem one, forsake it harshly and rudely? What have we in common with St. Bernard covering his eyes that they may not dwell upon the beauty of the lakes of Switzerland, or with the violent rhetoric of the Book of Revelation?"

Furthermore, consequences of dubious value follow upon this negative praxis. Since it requires the most heroic rejection of the common life, and enjoins the uncompromising progressive simplification of personal life at all levels of action, thinking, feeling, and willing, this way lies open only to the virtuoso. It is not a way for all men. As Schweitzer points out, it is a way for monks. "Now to what end did we come into religion," confesses Augustine Baker, "but only to avoid all these impediments of the world which withdraw us from attending to God . . . noise, tumults, and unavoidable distractions." The modern exponents of this path even speak of those who follow it as a biological mutation, a rare new species which appears only once in many millions of births. It is not surprising to discover, therefore, that the social theory which accompanies this form of piety is invariably nondemocratic and hierarchic. The caste structures of India and medieval Europe are significant examples.

There is reasonable doubt, furthermore, that the claims of this type of mysticism can be made good. It teaches that through a progressive abstraction from life the devotee will come at last to God in Himself. But is abstraction the way to God? "We must not try to uncreate the world in order to find God," insists Inge. "We were created out of nothing, but we cannot return to nothing to find our Creator there." More forcefully he asserts: "The explanation of the blank trance as a temporary transit into the Absolute must be set down as a pure delusion."

If it is not a way to God, is it a way to Unity? Although there seems to be no question that in Samadhi and Nirvana as taught by Vedantists and Buddhists the self finds a one-pointedness of concentrated being, Martin Buber, who practiced this type of religion for many years, protests calling it a state of union. Such spiritual exercises point to a oneness beyond time and space which may be experienced by the skilled practitioner when he turns his back upon the rest of life. But such union is in reality a splitting off from The Unity, leaving the everyday world streaming on to death while the mystic escapes into the fullness of ecstatic trance. In such a state, Buber testifies, the "religious" lifted you out. "Over there now lay the accustomed existence with its affairs, but here illumination, and ectasy and rapture held, without time or sequence. Thus your own being encompassed a life here and a life beyond, and there was no bond but the actual moment of the transition." In *Between Man and Man* he writes of his "conversion" from a spirituality which thus divides the temporal life from eternity and of his turning to a path which finds the Eternal "only in the fulfilling of . . . temporality," the living of a complete life of human responsibility and dialogue with his fellows amidst the ongoing course of affairs. Here in the context of humanity alone may man find God and discover a union which truly unites. The Christian symbol for this type of religiousness is the Incarnation.

Another hazard in the heroic praxis of abstractive mysticism is the temptation to pride or despair: pride if one succeeds to these high states of concentrated being, despair if one lacks the intelligence, physical equipment, or life circumstances to pursue the strenuous course to its conclusion.

And what of the effect upon human society? There is not space to detail a sociology of world-renouncing piety, but its dim view of the natural life, if widely adhered to, could not but make what we call civilization impossible. In the *Perennial Philosophy,* a compendium of mystical wisdom, excellent in so many ways, except, in my opinion, for its adherence to the negative tradition, Aldous Huxley writes of the natural world as "not merely the prelude and necessary condition of the Fall; to some extent it is the Fall." Elsewhere, in his *Ape and Essence,* he draws the inevitable conclusion concerning human destiny:

> Hope—
> Bless you little heart, there is no hope,
> Only the almost infinite probability
> Of consummating suddenly,
> Or else by agonizing inches
> The ultimate and irremediable
> Detumescence.

Contrast this with the Biblical story of creation in which "God saw . . . that . . . it was *very good,*" or the Psalmist's cry, "The earth is the Lord's and the *fulness* thereof," with its corollary, the coming of the Kingdom of God's righteousness.

In the following treatment of mystical prayer, everything is interpreted from the perspective of life-and-world-affirming mysticism. The problem is to draw off from the entire mystical tradition clues to the practice of prayer which lead to "fullness of Christ, and not the emptiness of the undifferentiated Godhead." This is not to say that every prayer and meditation need focus on Jesus. It is simply the recognition that the God to whom we pray is the Being who endlessly and everywhere pours Himself out as life, ever more life, and that the "event of Christ" is the Rosetta stone that enables us to decipher the meaning of that eternal outpouring. Unfortunately, the narrowing of Christianity into a rigid cult of the external Jesus has made him a problem for many sincere religious seekers, and serves to obscure the meaning of a Christocentric interpretation of prayer. To point my meaning here I can only indicate such contemporary interpretations of Christ as appear in the writings of Donald and John Baillie, Nels Ferré, Charles Raven, Paul Tillich, and the late Archbishop William Temple.

TYPES OF MYSTICAL PRAYER

The typically mystical methods of prayer parallel the threefold Way of mystical theology. During the purgative way, vocal prayer is the chief instrument. The attention of the easily distracted pilgrim is kept centered by the sound of his own voice and the reverberation through his nervous system of familiar symbols. On the illuminative way, mental prayer is used. Skilled visioning and discursive reasoning—all the devices described in the previous chapter—assist the mind in its Godward focus. Such prayer gradually gives way to occasional, and then more frequent, periods of rapt attention when thoughts and images die away and pure significance enfolds the mind. At last, in the unitive way, contemplative prayer emerges.

The three ascending levels of genuinely mystical prayer are:

affective prayer, the *prayer of simple regard*, and *"infused"* contemplation.

Affective prayer is primarily a work of the feelings. It is an
active direction of wholehearted and single-minded love toward
God. A fine guide to this type of devotion is the anonymous
author of *The Cloud of Unknowing*, a fourteenth-century manual of mystical piety. He advises that all sensual images, all
memories and thoughts be "trodden down under the cloud of
forgetting" until "nothing lives in the working mind but a
naked intent stretching to God." Entrenched in the Johannine
tradition of love as a means to the knowledge of God he writes:
"I would leave all the things about which I can think and choose
to love that about which I cannot, because He may be
fully loved who cannot be defined at all." "Such a blind shot
with the sharp dart of longing love," he promises, "may never
fail of the prick, the which is God."

Here discursive reasoning and imaginings are set aside. The
soul is content to sit quietly and reach for God with the heart
alone. God is beyond what we can think, but He is not beyond
being truly loved. "By love he may be gotten and holden, but
by the intellect never."

Should the ever-presumptuous intellect interrupt this colloquy,
The Cloud of Unknowing suggests an answer: "Have this intent
[to love alone] wrapped and enfolded in one word." Such a
word might be "God" or "love" and can be used as a rhythmic
drumbeat to focus the intention and drive off vagrant reflections.
The Puritan, Richard Baxter, suggests a similar solution: "Mix
ejaculations with thy cogitations and soliloquies till. . . . thou
hast pleaded thyself from a clod to a flame, from a forgetful
sinner to a mindful lover."

The *prayer of simplicity*, or *simple regard*, is so named because
it is an even more drastic simplification than affective prayer
which has already dispensed with images and reasonings. A fine

description of the prayer of simplicity appears in the *Guide to True Peace*, a manual popular among Quakers in the eighteenth century: "The sort of prayer to which we have alluded is that of inward silence; wherein the soul, abstracted from all outward things, in holy stillness, humble reverence, and lively faith, waits patiently to feel the Divine presence, and to receive the precious influence of the Holy Spirit. And when you retire for this purpose, which should be your frequent practice, you should consider yourselves as being placed in the Divine presence, looking with a single eye to him, resigning yourselves entirely into his hands, to receive from him whatsoever he may be pleased to dispense to you; calmly endeavouring, at the same time, to fix your mind in peace and silence; quitting all your own reasonings, and not willingly thinking on any thing, how good and how profitable soever it may appear to be. And should any vain thoughts present themselves, you should gently turn from them; and thus faithfully and patiently wait to feel the Divine presence."

The more cryptic words of T. S. Eliot are:

I said to my soul, be still, and wait without hope
For hope would be hope for the wrong thing; wait without love
For love would be love of the wrong thing; there is yet faith
But the faith and the love and the hope are all in the waiting.
Wait without thought, for you are not ready for thought:
So the darkness shall be the light, and the stillness the dancing.

This silence is a hard discipline and sorely tries our trust. As our own activity in prayer subsides, the sickening feeling that nothing is happening washes over us. But, surely, if prayer is a dialogue of Spirit, listening is as important as speaking, passivity as activity. This passivity is not dull or torpid but alert and watchful for the slightest intimations of the Spirit. In the midst of such listening, hope will rise, and love, and faith, but, as Eliot has warned, we must wait in the darkness and in the stillness.

Too great eagerness, out of lack of faith, leads to the pitiful and forlorn effort of spinning spiritual substance out of one's own soul.

"Infused contemplation," the third level of mystical prayer, is so named because the pray-er suddenly moves into experiences which he cannot consciously produce by an act of will. He is simply carried forward by the inflowing stream of light. At this exalted stage of prayer the acts of will so necessary in earlier stages are no longer needed. It was perhaps to such a sublime moment that the poet Wordsworth referred in his "Lines Composed a Few Miles Above Tintern Abbey" when he wrote of

> that blessed mood,
> In which the burthen of the mystery,
> In which the heavy and weary weight
> Of all this unintelligible world
> Is lightened—that serene and blessed mood
> In which the affections gently lead us on—
> Until, the breath of this corporeal frame
> And even the motion of our human blood
> Almost suspended, we are laid asleep
> In body, and become a living soul;
> While with an eye made quiet by the power
> Of harmony, and the deep power of joy,
> We see into the life of things.

St. Augustine, in one of the most moving passages of his *Confessions,* describes a conversation between himself and his mother as they waited in the port of Ostia for her passage home. Not then knowing that her voyage would be a journey into the next life, they stood at a window overlooking the garden of their house and talked intimately of the life of God in their experience. They spoke of His beauty in the created world and His yet more wondrous loveliness beyond their eyes. The Spirit seemed to lift them into a heavenly realm, "that region of never-failing plenty, *where Thou feedest Israel.*" They spoke of silencing the tumult of the flesh, silencing all the images of earth and heaven, and even silencing the soul herself, that they "might hear Whom in all these things we love, might hear His Very Self."

He then describes the culmination of this upward ascent in these words: "Could this be continued on, and other visions of kind far unlike be withdrawn, and this one ravish, and absorb, and wrap up its beholder amid these inward joys, so that life might be for ever like that one moment of understanding which now we sighed after: were not this, 'Enter into the joy of the Lord!' "

At this level of high prayer, the mystic says, the mysterious "oneing" of man and God transpires. What does he mean? What may we expect if we pursue the path of communion to its end?

THE UNITIVE STATE

At moments, in and out of prayer, there comes an accord to the human soul that can only be called a complete willingness that God's will be done in all and through all, a momentarily "undisturbed song of pure consent." The great Spanish mystic, St. John of the Cross, defines this "union of likeness" as the supernatural moment "when two wills, the will of God and the will of the soul, are conformed together, and neither desire aught repugnant to the other." In this state the soul "becomes transformed in God by love." Love is thus the measure of union, as all the great mystics have insisted. For, in the quaint words of *The Cloud of Unknowing,* it is essentially the work wherein is "knit up the ghostly knot of burning love betwext thee and thy God, in ghostly onehead and according of will."

There are unguarded moments in some mystical writings where the soul is said to be absorbed into God or to disappear in Him, but most Christian mystics make clear that they do not mean this literally. The identity is always a work of supernatural grace

whereby the creaturely will is purified by the holy Will of the
Creator. Against the monistic tendencies of most Asian mysticism *The Cloud of Unknowing* warns, "He is thy being, and
thou not His." The shoemaker mystic, Jacob Boehme, makes the
same point in an analogy. The soul united with God, he says, is
like a "bright flaming piece of iron, which of itself is dark and
black, and the fire so penetrateth and shineth through the iron,
that it giveth light." It is clear, he concludes, that "the iron doth
not cease to be; it is iron still."

But all our analogues are drawn from the realm of objects
where interpenetration is always limited by the fact that one
thing cannot exist in the same space with another. The interpenetration of Spirit is more intimate than the fire to Boehme's
shining white hot iron. Traditional conceptions of the separateness of personality would make impossible the interpenetration
of personhood which mystical union presupposes. But it is separation, not individuality, which forbids authentic union. Baron
von Hügel, grappling with this problem, wisely perceives that
God's action in the soul "will have to be conceived as operating
in and through and with our own; . . . finding in one sense its
very matter, in another, its very form, in our own free willings."
He suggests that we can all know by analogy from our experience of one another in friendship or love, that "God's Spirit ever
works in closest penetration and stimulation of our own; just as,
in return, we cannot find God's Spirit simply separate from our
own spirit within ourselves."

Here again, at the very culmination of the interior life, we
shall have to reject the principle of abstractive mysticism and
quietism, that the more there is of the Creator the less there is
of the creature, just as we must reject the materialistic analogy
which must ever have any one real thing outside another. The
incarnational view which, in my judgment, best fits the facts of
the religious life "finds," in the words of von Hügel, "spiritual

realities and forces working the one inside the other and through
the other."

Traditional treatises on the unitive life have concentrated
almost exclusively on the relationship between the individual
soul and God. I believe that the fullest union toward which we
should look is larger than that described by most of the mystics.
The whole of life, including our fellow men and nature, should
be brought within the perspective of this expectation. There is a
profound sense in which the union of any one person to God
is not fully consummated until all men are joined to Him as
well. Only in the realized Kingdom of God, when all things have
been subdued by His mighty working, is the Unity complete.
Without my brother I cannot come fully to God; this, not for the
reason that, as Max Müller thought, I and my brother are actually
one, but because the true Unity is a oneness of boundless love,
and such love is necessarily incomplete as long as anyone, however humanly insignificant or resistant, is left out.

A great seer of ancient Israel envisaged the Kingdom as a
universal melting of enmity, leading to endless harmony in the
natural world, restored by God:

> Then the wolf will lodge with the lamb
> And the leopard will lie down with the kid;
> The calf and the young lion will graze together,
> And a little child will lead them.
> . . . .
> For the Land will have become full of the knowl-
>   edge of the Lord,
> As the waters cover the sea.

The foregoing account of the unitive way confirms what has
been said before: the full life of prayer requires a judicious and
varied use of all the types of prayer treated in this work. Mystical
experiences which emerge during moments of affective prayer or

the prayer of simplicity are not the signal to abandon adoration, confession, or petition. If, as an early English contemplative promises, it should sometime happen in mystical elevation that God "send out a beam of spiritual light that will pierce this Cloud of unknowing that is between you and Him, and show you some of His hiddenness, which no man can describe," you should not conclude that all of life was aimed to just this moment, and that all the prayer which went before is an inferior form of spirituality. God is no more present to us when we attend to Him alone than when we attend to our neighbor in Him.

STATES ACCOMPANYING THE PRACTICE OF INTERIOR PRAYER

The path from purgation to union is not plain. Sometimes the illuminative period abounds in strange visions, ecstasies, and other psychic states. Depending upon the form they take, they may be comforting or distracting. In their happier guise they offer a strong temptation to the pilgrim to tarry at the inn. If a voice begins to communicate strange and wonderful messages, it may take great manliness of spirit to brush it aside and press on to a higher calling. Visions, supernatural intuitions, revelations, and disclosures of mysteries will seem too sacred, important, and, above all, pleasant, to set aside in order to resume the more cheerless task of growth in charity. "Faith and love," chides St. John of the Cross, "are better than interior voices." And perfection, the saints remind us, lies not in high thoughts or sweet feelings.

This does not mean that there is anything evil or wrong in these experiences. They must be recognized as by-products of a more serious enterprise, accepted as they come, but not clung to or prized for themselves. From clinging to these experiences it is but a short step into the occult, where supernatural powers and esoteric lore beckon the unwary. I have no word on the value of research into occult regions, except to point out that it is not in the direct line of spiritual growth. Whatever justification it may have derives from is problematic kinship to science by way of ESP and Psychic Research rather than from religion.

If sometimes the mystic path leads through visions and ecstasies, at others it wanders in desert places. Sensible comforts of prayer are withdrawn, and satisfactions in devotion are replaced by a complete distaste for religious exercises. This is the phenomenon known as "dryness." The soul that has been traveling forward rapidly under full sail before the wind of the Spirit suddenly finds himself becalmed in the horse latitudes. How easy, then, to believe that God has abandoned him. Old doubts, thought long dead, arise to haunt his cheerless devotions. George Fox, founder of the Society of Friends, had such an experience as he was sitting one morning by the fire. His *Journal* reads: "A great cloud came over me, a temptation beset me; and I sat still. It was said, All things come by Nature; and the elements and stars came over me, so that I was in a manner quite clouded by it." He wisely waited in patience, not fighting the vision nor attempting to drive it away. Then he reports: "At last a living hope and a true voice arose in me, which said, There is a living God who made all things. Immediately the cloud and temptation vanished away, and life rose over it all."

After many such skirmishes with dryness the mystic finally, at the highest level of interior prayer, suffers the onset of what has been called "the dark night of the soul," a period of utter stagnation so far as mystical activity is concerned. Former powers fall away and impotence, blankness, and solitude abide. Why should this take place?

One reason, no doubt, is that rigorous spiritual cultivation is subject to the same laws of fatigue and nervous reaction which govern all highly intense forms of creative activity. The Blessed Henry Suso says that his "jubilation and internal joys . . . all had to be paid for afterward with great suffering." The dark night, like the spells of dryness which preceded it, can in part be traced to a natural exhaustion of the overstrained nervous system.

Another partial explanation for these negative reactions which interrupt prayer is an imbalance in personal growth. Intense spirituality often drives a man to neglect aspects of his life. It also inclines him to repress those forces in his personality which resist spiritual progress. The time comes when these unrecognized segments of life must be accounted for. The spearhead of prayer must wait for the troops to catch up. God wants to bring to Himself the whole man, not just the idealized fragments. The stalled advance in prayer is not a dead loss provided we do not give up, but allow the slow inner ripening to proceed at its own pace, recognizing that it may be many months or even years before the imbalance has been made good.

Exploring the nature of personality yet further, we discover another source of the dark night. Considering the social components in personality, the way in which culture enters into the very texture of thought and feeling, and coupling this consideration with the fact of the distance of human culture from the ideals of the Kingdom of God, it is no wonder that the soul intent upon seeking Him and His Kingdom first is going to suffer extreme tension. This tension will return in one form or another at every level of prayer. At some levels it will appear with greater and more impenetrable darkness than at others. And whenever the Spirit's demand becomes one of total commitment, self-giving, and self-abandonment, the most immense forces of opposition make their simultaneous appearance from every region of life.

Some of the suffering recorded by the saints no doubt also stems from a too great dependence upon the principles of abstractive piety. The devotee of such a regimen is struggling not only with actual dark resistances to God's will but also with the innocent and outraged powers within himself. He is plagued by loneliness, starved affections, languishing talents, and a body outraged by overstrain and undercare. The Christian mystic is also a very sensitive member of society, who, despite his theories of retirement from the world, cannot but hear the cries of suffering induced by social neglect and misused power. Allan Hunter questions whether the dark night suffered by the Spanish St. John may not have been deepened by a pall of smoke from the smoldering bodies of heretics burned by the Inquisition.

This account of the dryness and dark night attendant upon mystical prayer suggests certain practical observations. First, a moderate pace is called for. Evelyn Underhill sums it up: "We are required to be reasonable both in what we refuse to nature and what we demand from it; temperate in renunciation as well as enjoyment, in super-sensible as well as sensible activities." Second, during the slack periods, prayer should be continued however distasteful it may be. Such waiting on God without any sensible response is a salutary medicine for egotism. It weans us away from the enjoyment of God for His gifts to a steady affection for Him in Himself. A return to simpler modes of prayer is also prescribed. Loyola recommended for such barren times the use of rhythmical vocal prayer. It requires little mental effort and the drumbeat carries attention forward almost automatically. Another salutary prescription is a return to the average practice of the common religious life of the community with its adaptation to ordinary needs and limitations.

A final suggestion is that the prayer of communion should be more perfectly related to the entire work of God in nature, in history, and in other persons. Its practice should not be a hard driving lunge toward a final state of unitive rest, but a continuous enlargement of the soul into the whole of life, gathering more and more of it up, as God allows, into an Eternal significance. Under this regime personal suffering will not cease. But

P

instead of the complaints of the dark night—apathy, dullness, and indifference—there will be the strain of holy living in an unholy world. We will experience the meaning of Christ's words, "I have a baptism to undergo—what tension I suffer till it is all over." At the mature levels of the incarnational life suffering and joy will alternate, not with the soul's pulse and temperature, but with the tasks and resolutions of the ongoing Kingdom.

THE PRACTICE OF THE PRESENCE OF GOD

In the *Tales of the Hasidim,* the Baal Shem is reported to have said: "Imagine a man whose business hounds him through many streets and across the market-place the livelong day. He almost forgets there is a Maker of the world. Only when the time for the Afternoon Prayer comes, does he remember: 'I must pray.' And then, from the bottom of his heart, he heaves a sigh of regret that he has spent his day on vain and idle matters, and he runs into a by-street and stands there, and prays: God holds him dear, very dear and his prayer pierces the firmament." This is what the set time of prayer can mean, a recollection of true Being, nullifying the scattering influence of the market-place.

A life of faithfulness to a well-conceived rule of daily prayer will in the course of time build the foundations for what St. Paul calls prayer "without ceasing." Here the thought of God is never absent from at least one of the many layers of consciousness, and throughout the day, either as a conscious act or as a background of awareness, there proceeds a ceaseless bowing down in humble adoration to the living God. Nicholas Herman of Lorraine, a seventeenth-century Carmelite, better known as Brother Lawrence, gave this type of praying its name and definition. "I make it my only business," he writes in his Sixth Letter, "to persevere in His Holy Presence, wherein I keep my self by a simple attention and an absorbing passionate regard to God, which I may call an actual Presence of God; to speak better; a silent and secret, constant intercourse of the soul with God."

This state of constant collectedness was not attained at a bound. After ten years of intense fluctuating devotion during which the Presence was felt only during seasons of prayer, or only as an occasional and fleeting interruption of normal pre-occupations, he arrived at this skilled attention which never seemed afterward to flag. The practice of the Presence of God had become constant.

Those who observed him were more convinced of his habitual spiritual communion by his manner and bearing than by his words. The author of some "Conversations" with Brother Lawrence records: "His countenance was edifying, such a sweet and calm devotion, appearing in it as could not but affect the beholders. And it was observed that in the greatest hurry of business in the kitchen [for fifteen years he was the monastery's cook, work he abhorred but accepted for the love of God] he still preserved his recollection and heavenly-mindedness. He was never hasty nor loitering, but did each thing in its season, with an even uninterrupted composure and tranquillity of spirit. 'The time of business,' said he, 'does not with me differ from the time of prayer, and in the noise and clatter of my kitchen, while several persons are at the same time calling for different things, I possess God in as great tranquillity as if I were upon my knees at the blessed sacrament.'"

Brother Lawrence did all his work, even that of picking up straws from the ground, for the love of God. This he coupled with a "hearty renunciation of everything which we are sensible does not lead to God." When practicing some virtue he would occasionally address God by saying, "Lord, I cannot do this unless Thou enable me." His biographer writes that "he was very sensible of his faults, but not discouraged by them." When he was conscious of his faults, he would confess them humbly to God, but "he did not plead against Him to excuse them. When he had so confessed, he peaceably resumed his usual practice of love and adoration."

One feature of Brother Lawrence's piety needs comment. "I have quitted all forms of devotion and set prayers," he confesses in his Sixth Letter, "save those to which my state obliges me." When, many years ago, I discovered this technique of praying without interruption to the ordinary course of activities, I thought of it as a fine way to save the time and trouble of special prayer periods. This presumptuous experiment in continual prayer collapsed as soon as it began. The practice of the Presence cannot be employed as a device for reducing prayer to a secondary activity which no longer interferes with other "more important" things. The expanding demands upon spiritual vitality in dynamic modern society make giving up set exercises and times for prayer exceedingly dubious. As this environment demands more and more of us as workers, parents, or administrators, we are met constantly with material which needs to be "worked up" in skillful prayer. As unideal as Brother Lawrence's life in the monastery may have been, it had a stability and predictability about it, even set times for group worship and silence, which are not available to most men in modern circumstances. We will, therefore, no doubt find it more advantageous to undertake his practice of the Presence without substituting it for the disciplines of set prayer.

Our Lord, with all the intensity of the Presence about him, did not give over seasons of prayer, but was often discovered spending the night or early hours of the day for this purpose. And at the end, when his betrayer had to designate a place for the arrest, it was Jesus' habit of prayer which enabled Judas to name Gethsemane.

A modern teacher of the practice of continual prayer is Frank Laubach, whose missionary career has been noted earlier. His *Letters by a Modern Mystic*, written while alone on an island in the Philippines, record the initiation of his own experiment with this type of awareness. On January 26, 1930, he wrote: "For the past few days I have been experimenting in a more complete surrender than ever before. I am taking by deliberate act of will enough time from each hour to give God much thought. Yesterday and today I have made a new adventure, which is not easy to express. I am feeling God in each movement, by an act of will—willing that He shall direct these fingers that now strike this typewriter—willing that He shall pour through my steps as I walk—willing that He shall direct my words as I speak, my very jaws as I eat!"

At the end of this year of experimentation he began to broaden his work and to accept very heavy responsibilities. In the light of this new kind of life he found a new development in the practice of ceaseless prayer. On September 28, 1931, he wrote: "Last year, as you know, I decided to try to keep God in mind all the time. That was rather easy for a lonesome man in a strange land. It has always been easier for the shepherds, and the monks, and anchorites than for people surrounded by crowds.

"But today is an altogether different thing. I am no longer lonesome. The hours of the day from dawn to bedtime are spent in the presence of others. Either this new situation will crowd God out or I must take him into it all. I must learn a continuous silent conversation of heart to heart with God while looking into other eyes and listening to other voices. If I decide to do this it is far more difficult than the thing I was doing before.

"Yet if this experiment is to have any value for busy people it must be worked under exactly these conditions of high pressure and throngs of people.

"There is only one way to do it. God must share my thoughts of Moro grammar, and Moro epics, and type, and teaching people to read, and talking over the latest excitement with my family as we read the newspapers. So I am resolved to let nothing, nothing, stop me from this effort save sheer fatigue that stops all thought."

The intention in this practice of continual prayer, bridging the space between set times of devotion, is to sense the relevance of Eternity to so many times and places that referring every thought and feeling to God becomes a continuous habit, to realize finally that the holy, as Paul Tillich teaches, is a dimension in everything real, not a section within reality. As this relaxed effort of attention is practiced, failure will occur less and less often. Slowly, quite imperceptibly, the whole life is gathered up to Him. This is what St. Paul calls the "mind of Christ." All those little inner "deaths" to chaos and self-will are followed by the mysterious "resurrections" in which the "new being" that was Jesus Christ begins to shine through the opaque material of human life and transform it.

Prayer and the study of prayer is endless. In his last days, at the crown of his sanctity. St. Francis, bearing in his body the wounds of the stigmata and in his spirit the unmistakable marks of divine charity, was accustomed to say to his followers, "Let us *begin*, Brethren, to serve our Lord God, for until now we have made but little progress." We are thus always at the beginning, and by the paradox of grace, we are always at the end.

We have traced our understanding of prayer and reality from adoration of the transcendent Unity to the intimate life of communion with the Father who empties Himself and dwells with us as a Son. We have understood prayer as the life of God joined to man, not only in the high moments of inspiration but in the tedious hours of the commonplace. This is the secret: Incarnation.

> Here the impossible union
> Of spheres of existence is actual.

Such is the holy mystery which God offers in prayer. How can we do other than turn to Him in glad conspiring reception?

NOTES

Notes

Unless otherwise noted Biblical references are to the Revised Standard Version of the Bible, copyrighted 1946 and 1952 by the Division of Christian Education of the National Council of the Churches of Christ in America.

CHAPTER 1. *Prayer, the Church, and Society*

PAGE	LINE	
2	3	"The Rock," in T. S. Eliot, *The Complete Poems and Plays, 1909-1950* (Faber & Faber). Used by permission.
2	20	*Idem.*
3	30	Mother Juliana of Norwich, *Revelations of Divine Love*, Dom Roger Hudleston, ed. (Burns, Oates).
4	1	Charles Hendel, *Civilization and Religion* (New Haven: Yale University Press).
4	7	Max Weber, *The Protestant Ethic and the Spirit of Capitalism*, tr. Talcott Parsons (Allen & Unwin). In support of this same thesis, see also R. H. Tawney, *Religion and the Rise of Capitalism* (John Mang).
4	11	Hendel, *op. cit.*
4	20	Isa. 6:5.

PAGE	LINE	
4	24	W. H. Auden and Christopher Isherwood, *Journey to a War* (Faber & Faber). Used by permission.
5	5	"For You, O Democracy."
7	18	Graham Greene, *The Power and the Glory* (Heinemann).
8	24	Frankel-Brunswik, Levinson, and Sanford, "The Antidemocratic Personality," in G. E. Swanson, Theodore Newcomb, and Eugene Hartley, *Readings in Social Psychology* (New York: Henry Holt).
9	5	A. H. Maslow, "Love in Healthy People," in Ashley Montagu, *The Meaning of Love* (New York: Julian).
10	2	Greene, *op. cit.*
10	11	From "Orion," Aldous Huxley, *The Cicadas in Verses and a Comedy* (Chatto & Windus). Used by permission.

CHAPTER 2. *Science, Law, and Prayer*

12	28	T. S. Eliot, *Four Quartets* (Faber & Faber). Used by permission.
13	30	Alfred North Whitehead, *Science and the Modern World* (Cambridge University Press).
14	1	Max Planck, *The Universe in the Light of Modern Physics* (New York: W. W. Norton).
14	10	Cited by A. S. Eddington, *New Pathways in Science* (Cambridge University Press).
14	28	*Ibid.*
15	3	*Idem.*
15	9	For a summary of this evidence, see Karl Heim, *The Transformation of the Scientific World View* (New York: Harper).
15	13	Whitehead, *op. cit.*
16	8	Heim, *op. cit.*, develops this view of natural law with high faithfulness to the scientific data.
16	11	*Ibid.*
17	12	Whitehead, *op. cit.*
17	16	*Ibid.*
19	11	For data on these experiments, see J. B. Rhine, *The Reach of the Mind* (New York: William Sloane), chap. four.
19	25	Heim, *op. cit.*
20	4	*Ibid.*
20	25	Mark 11:23.
20	29	Heim, *op. cit.*
21	6	*Ibid.*
21	25	Mark 11:24.

PAGE   LINE
22   8   A. S. Eddington, *The Nature of the Physical World* (Cambridge University Press).
24   33   Whitehead, *op. cit.*
25   4   *Ibid.*
25   7   Cited by J. W. N. Sullivan, *The Limitations of Science* (New York: New American Library).
26   8   Whitehead, *op. cit.*
26   19   *Ibid.*
26   24   Cited by Sullivan, *op. cit.*
27   1   Max Planck, "Causality in Physics," in Norbert Wiener, ed., *Readings in the Philosophy of Science* (New York: Scribner's).
27   22   Cited by Sullivan, *op. cit.*
28   2   Bertrand Russell, "Science and Value," in Wiener, *op. cit.*
28   25   *Idem.*
28   33   *Idem.*

CHAPTER 3. *The Problem of Unanswered Prayer*

31   12   James 4:3.
31   14   John Gaynor Banks, *The Basic Laws of Spiritual Therapy* (London Healing Mission).
31   30   Mark 9:29.
33   4   Mark 6:5.
33   11   1 Cor. 15:58 (Phillips).
33   23   This expression is used by Rudolph Otto in *The Idea of the Holy* (Oxford University Press).
35   7   2 Cor. 12:9 (AV).
35   9   Rom. 9:1 (Phillips).
35   28   Mother Juliana of Norwich, *op. cit.*
35   30   Luke 18:1 (Moffatt).
36   5   Eliot, *Four Quartets* (Faber & Faber). Used by permission

CHAPTER 4. *The Spectrum of Prayer*

37   1   "Adonais."
38   32   Isa. 6:1.
40   16   Phil. 2:12-13 (AV).
40   32   Cited by Alan Watts, *The Supreme Identity* (New York: Pantheon).
41   19   Luke 12:32.
41   27   Ps. 139:8.
42   10   Eliot, *Four Quartets* (Faber & Faber). Used by permission.

PAGE	LINE	
42	28	Geraldine Coster, *Yoga and Western Psychology* (Oxford University Press).
43	3	Luke 17:21.
43	6	Luke 11:20.

CHAPTER 5. *The Starting Point: God Is God*

44	1	1 Chron. 29:11.
44	11	Cited by F. E. Christmas, ed., *Hear My Prayer* (Hodder & Stoughton).
44	17	Italics mine.
45	25	Ps. 93 (Moffatt).
46	18	Job 40:4.
46	20	Job 42:3-6.
47	2	*The Bhagavad Gita*, trs. Swami Prabhavanda and Christopher Isherwood (Phoenix House).
47	33	Lao Tse, *The Tao Teh Ching*, tr. Lin Yutang, in Lin Yutang, ed., *The Wisdom of China and India* (Michael Joseph).
48	2	John Hutchinson has added the word "intimate" to Paul Tillich's basic term.
48	10	Ps. 139 (Moffatt).
50	7	Eph. 4:6.
50	15	Logan Pearsall Smith, *All Trivia* (Constable).
50	32	Fred Hoyle, *The Nature of the Universe* (Blackwell).
51	9	Martin Buber, *I and Thou* (T. & T. Clark).
51	18	*Ibid.*
52	33	Eph. 4:20.
53	3	Buber, *op. cit.*
53	7	In Paul Keigley, *The Theology of Paul Tillich* (New York: Macmillan).
53	31	Exod. 33:20 (AV).
54	5	Buber, *op. cit.*
54	12	*Ibid.*

CHAPTER 6. *The Meaning of Confession*

55	14	Lev. 11:44.
55	15	Matt. 5:48.
56	6	Evelyn Underhill, *Mysticism* (Methuen).
56	27	Cited by Alan Watts, *Spirit of Zen* (John Murray).
57	28	Rabindranath Tagore, "Gitanjali," in *Collected Poems and Plays* (Macmillan). Used by permission of the publishers and the author's trustees.

PAGE	LINE	
59	3	Matt. 22:40.
59	8	1 John 4:16 (AV).
60	1	Charles Raven, *Natural Religion and Christian Theology* (Cambridge University Press).
60	7	Charles Hartshorne, *Reality and Social Process* (Boston: Beacon).
60	12	From "Songs of Innocence."
60	30	Rom. 8:26 (Phillips).
61	1	The philospher Charles Hartshorne has developed these ideas as the core of an entire philosophy of reality. See his *Vision of God, The Divine Relativity, Reality and Social Process,* and *Philosophers Speak of God.*
61	29	Matt. 5-8.
62	25	See Ashley Montagu, *On Being Human* (New York: Henry Schuman). See also his contribution to Montagu, ed., *The Meaning of Love* (Julian).
63	7	The research of Rene A. Spitz in French orphanages is cited by Montagu, *ibid.* On the increasing evidence from biology, medicine, psychiatry, and the social sciences for the curative and maturing power of love, see, among others: P. A. Sorokin, *Forms and Techniques of Altruistic and Spiritual Growth* (Boston: Beacon), and *The Ways and Power of Love* (Boston: Beacon).
63	9	Ashley Montagu, "The Origin and Meaning of Love," *Journal of Pastoral Psychology,* IV (June 1953).
63	14	Hartshorne, *op. cit.*
63	24	Montagu, "The Origin and Meaning of Love."
63	31	A. W. Loos, ed., *The Nature of Man* (New York: Church Peace Union).
64	9	Presidential address before the Pacific Division of the American Philosophical Association, Dec. 1953.
64	20	P. A. Sorokin, *The Reconstruction of Humanity* (Boston: Beacon).
64	31	Aldous Huxley, *The Perennial Philosophy* (Chatto & Windus).
65	10	Lewis Mumford, *In the Name of Sanity* (New York: Harcourt Brace).
65	21	See note for page 61, line 1.
66	13	H. F. Cary, tr.
66	26	*Idem.*
67	4	2 Cor. 13:9 (Phillips).
67	6	Methodist liturgy of the Holy Communion, composed of these references: 2 Pet. 1:3; Eph. 3:17, 19; and Rom. 6:5.
67	10	Eph. 4:15.

PAGE   LINE
67   24   These distinctions are made with great clarity and beauty by Buber, *op. cit.*
68   1   Fritz Kunkel, *In Search of Maturity* (New York: Scribner's).
69   6   John 1:12.
69   10   John 1:14 (AV).
69   10   Col. 1:16 (AV).
69   15   1 Cor. 15:31.
69   16   Gal. 2:20 (AV).
69   23   Rom. 8:29 and Heb. 2:11.
69   25   Rom. 8:15 (AV).

CHAPTER 7. *The Method of Confession*

70   9   *George Fox, An Autobiography*, Rufus Jones, ed. (Philadelphia: Ferris & Leach).
71   26   Ps. 139:19.
72   16   Fox, *op. cit.*
72   27   Lewis Maclachlan, *Intelligent Prayer* (James Clarke).
72   32   *Ibid.*
73   24   *Hamlet*, Act III, sc. iii.
74   26   Coster, *op. cit.*
74   33   *Ibid.*
75   31   William James' phrase.
76   18   Jean Pierre Camus, *The Spirit of St. Francis de Sales* (Longmans).
77   23   Jer. 15:15-19.
78   29   Kunkel, *op. cit.*
79   14   *Ibid.*
83   11   From a sermon in *Temple Tidings* (London: City Temple, Feb., 1954).
84   6   "Uphill."
84   11   Cited by Douglas Steere. *Doors into Life* (New York: Harper).
85   11   Col. 2:16-23 (Phillips).
85   14   Italics mine.
85   33   Luke 18:23.
86   2   Anatole France, *Le Puits de Sainte Claire.*
86   21   Phil. 4:12.
87   2   Matt. 11:16-19.

CHAPTER 8. *The Application of Confession*

90   6   Karen Horney, *Neurosis and Human Growth* (New York: W. W. Norton).

PAGE	LINE	
90	18	*Ibid.*
90	32	*Ibid.*
91	17	*Ibid.*
91	19	*Ibid.*
91	27	*Ibid.*
91	30	*Ibid.*
92	3	*Ibid.*
92	5	*Ibid.*
92	15	Rufus Jones, *The Testimony of the Soul* (New York: Macmillan).
92	22	*Ibid.*
93	16	Horney, *op. cit.*
93	23	For a standard account, see Percival M. Symonds, *Dynamics of Human Adjustment* (New York: Appleton-Century).
96	33	Rom. 8:28.
98	24	Juliana of Norwich, *op. cit.*
101	6	Maslow, *op. cit.*
101	20	C. S. Lewis, *That Hideous Strength* (Geoffrey Bles).
101	24	C. S. Lewis, "The Inner Ring," in *The Weight of Glory* (Geoffrey Bles).
102	19	Horney, *op. cit.*
103	28	Matt. 8:20.
104	22	D. C. Somervell abridgment of Arnold Toynbee, *A Study of History* (Oxford University Press), chaps. 16 and 19.
104	28	Gerald Heard, *Gabriel and the Creatures* (New York: Harper).
105	14	1 John 3:2.
105	20	Martin Buber, ed., *Tales of the Hasidim* (New York: Schocken Books), II.
106	4	2 Kings 16:10-16.
106	17	1 Kings 18:21 (Moffatt).
106	18	Matt. 6:22 (AV).
106	29	Toynbee, *op. cit.*, chaps. 16 and 19.
107	4	Jer. 17 (Moffatt).
110	20	J. P. de Caussade, *Abandonement to Divine Providence* (New York: Benziger).
110	23	Reported to the author in private conversation by a student of Dr. Kunkel.
110	28	De Caussade, *op. cit.*
111	16	*Ibid.*
111	19	*Ibid.*
111	31	*Ibid.*

PAGE	LINE	
112	2	*Ibid.*
112	3	*Ibid.*
112	14	Cited by Phillips, *op. cit.*
112	21	De Caussade, *op. cit.*
112	23	*Ibid.*

CHAPTER 9. *Petition and God's Creativity*

113	3	Andrew Murray, *With Christ in the School of Prayer* (New York: Revell).
113	5	Matt. 21:22.
113	14	Smiley Blanton, "Analytical Study of a Cure at Lourdes," *The Psychoanalytic Quarterly*, 9 (1940).
115	23	Gen. 1:1.
115	29	Rom. 8:28.
115	30	John 5:17.
116	11	Hoyle, *op cit.*
118	23	Cited by Hornell Hart, *The Technique of Social Progress* (New York: Henry Holt).
118	29	*Ibid.*
119	2	Brewster Ghiselin, *The Creative Process* (Berkeley: University of California Press).
119	26	*Ibid.*
120	1	*Ibid.*
120	8	Cited by E. D. Hutchinson, *How to Think Creatively* (New York: Abingdon).
120	17	*Ibid.*
121	5	Ghiselin, *op. cit.*
122	25	From "The Answer", *The Selected Poetry of Robinson Jeffers* (New York: Random House). Used by permission.
123	8	Juliana of Norwich, *op. cit.*
123	19	Cited in Emil Brunner, *Christianity and Civilization* (Nisbet).
123	21	*Ibid.*

CHAPTER 10. *A Pattern of Petition*

126	5	Joanna Field, *A Life of One's Own* (Chatto & Windus).
126	13	*Ibid.*
127	5	*The Teachings of the Compassionate Buddha.* E. A. Burtt, ed. (New York: New American Library).
127	10	Matt. 7:7 (AV).
127	12	Matt. 7:11 (AV).
127	13	Matt. 6:32 (AV).

PAGE	LINE	
127	17	This theme is developed by Carl Jung in several of his works, especially in *Modern Man in Search of a Soul, Psychology and Religion, The Integration of Personality,* and (with Richard Wilhelm) *The Secret of the Golden Flower.*
127	18	Carl Sandburg, *The People, Yes* (New York: Harcourt Brace). Used by permission.
127	27	Edgar Sheffield Brightman, *A Philosophy of Religion* (New York: Prentice-Hall).
128	17	J. B. Rhine, "Psi Phenomena and Psychiatry," *Proceedings of the Royal Society of Medicine,* 43 (Nov., 1950).
128	32	Norman Vincent Peale and Smiley Blanton, *Faith Is the Answer* (World's Work).
129	12	Rhine, *op. cit.*
130	23	Mary Austin, *Can Prayer be Answered?* (New York: Farrar & Rinehart).
131	10	*Ibid.*
132	27	John 14:14 (AV).
132	28	John 15:16 (AV).
132	29	John 15:7 (AV).
132	30	Matt. 6:33 (AV).
133	21	*Sacred Books of the World,* ed. and author A. C. Bouquet (Penguin Books).
134	3	Juliana of Norwich, *op. cit.* Used by permission.
135	7	Mark 11:24.
135	9	Mark 9:23.
135	12	In a lecture at Camp Menucha, Oregon, summer of 1952.
135	29	1 Cor. 3:21, 23.
136	9	Rom. 8:28.
136	11	Jer. 31:3 (AV).
136	12	Ps. 103:2-5.
136	16	Jer. 32:27.
136	21	Heb. 11:1.
136	22	Mark 11:24.
136	23	1 John 5:14.
136	25	Rom. 8:28.
136	30	Matt. 8:5.
137	4	Mark 14:28.
137	27	Two good introductions to this subject are Wendell Johnson, *People in Quandaries* (New York: Harper), and Irving J. Lee, *Language Habits in Human Affairs* (New York: Harper).
138	12	Deut. 4:32.
139	2	*A Midsummer Night's Dream,* Act V, sc. i.

Q

PAGE	LINE	
139	10	Luke 17:21.
139	10	Luke 11:20.
139	23	Glenn Clark, *I Will Lift Up Mine Eyes* (Arthur Jones), chap. 3.
140	14	Luke 22:42.
140	24	St. John of the Cross, *The Complete Works of Saint John of the Cross*, tr. David Lewis (Longmans), I.
140	30	From a metrical composition known as "Hsin-hsin-ming," or "Inscribed on the Believing Mind." The entire poem is cited by D. T. Suzuki, *Essays in Zen Buddhism* (Rider).
141	1	Matt. 16:25.
141	24	*A Book of Jewish Thoughts*, Joseph Herman Hertz, ed., (New York: Bloch).
142	19	Otto, *op. cit.*
143	17	*The Dialogues of Plato*, tr. Benjamin Jowett.
143	22	Evelyn Underhill, *Worship* (Nisbet).

CHAPTER 11. *Enlarging the Circle of Grace through Intercession*

144	6	Rom. 8:26 (AV).
145	15	E. Herman, *Creative Prayer* (James Clark).
146	19	Whitehead, *op. cit.*
147	14	Leslie D. Weatherhead deals with the question of whether prayer is merely telepathy in his chapter, "Intercession," in *Psychology, Religion and Healing* (Hodder & Stoughton).
147	17	Rhine, *op. cit.*
148	3	*Ibid.*
148	25	*Ibid.*
149	33	Austin, *op. cit.*
150	16	1 John 3:14.
151	14	Cited by E. Underhill, in Christmas, *op. cit.*
156	5	Henrick Ibsen, *Peer Gynt.*
157	8	Weatherhead, *op. cit.*
158	23	Louise Eggleston, *A Challenge to Christians* (Norfolk, Virginia: World Literacy Prayer Group).

CHAPTER 12. *Problem-solving Prayer*

160	4	Brand Blanshard's expression.
160	16	Chuangtse, in Lin Yutang, *op. cit.*
162	3	Stewart Edward White, *Across the Unknown* (New York: Dutton).
162	24	*The Bible of the World*, Robert O. Ballou, ed. (Routledge).

PAGE	LINE	
163	15	Eccles. 3:11.
165	20	Rufus Moseley, *Manifest Victory* (New York: Harper).
166	10	Edmund Jacobson, *Progressive Relaxation* (Chicago: University of Chicago Press). He popularized these ideas in *You Must Relax* (New York: Pocket Books).
166	31	2 Cor. 10:5.
167	26	Austin, *op. cit.*
168	18	White, *op cit.*
169	8	In a talk given on May 7, 1940, to divinity students at Bishop's Hostel, Lincoln, England.
169	24	Heim, *op. cit.*
170	11	*Ibid.*
171	1	J. B. Rhine in the *American Weekly*, March 20, 1952. Taken from Eldon Roark, *Just a Mutt* (New York: McGraw-Hill).
171	31	William J. Johnstone, *How Lincoln Prayed* (New York: Abingdon).
172	3	William J. Johnstone, *Abraham Lincoln, the Christian* (New York: Eaton and Mains).
172	23	1 John 4:1 (AV).

CHAPTER 13. *Commitment and Thanksgiving*

174	2	John Nicholas Grou, *Manual for Interior Souls* (St. Anselm's Society).
174	7	*Ibid.*
175	13	*Theologia Germanica*, Thomas Kepler, ed. (New York: World Publishing Co.).
175	22	Cited by Steere, *op. cit.*
175	27	*The Divine Comedy*, "Hell," canto iii.
176	22	Ps. 92:1, 2 (Moffatt).
176	28	Paul Sabatier, *Life of St. Francis of Assisi* (New York: Scribner's).
177	24	John 11:41.
178	10	Ps. 116:1, 2 (Moffatt).
178	21	Rev. 4:11.

CHAPTER 14. *Finding Reality through Meditation*

180	14	Bede Frost, *Art of Mental Prayer* (Philip Allan).
180	18	Adolphe Tanquery, *The Spiritual Life* (Tournai, Belgium: Desclee).
181	14	Luke 5:17.
182	21	Albert Schweitzer proposes this concept in lieu of Descartes' celebrated "I think, therefore, I am."

PAGE	LINE	
184	3	Gerald Heard, *Prayers and Meditations* (New York: Harper).
184	20	Evelyn Underhill, *Practical Mysticism* (J. M. Dent).
185	1	Field, *op. cit.*
185	14	Eliot, *Four Quartets* (Faber & Faber). Used by permission.
187	2	Her story is told in Julia de Beausobre, *The Woman That Could Not Die* (Gollancz).
188	16	James Martineau, *Endeavours After the Christian Life* (New York: Longmans).
189	6	Evelyn Underhill, *The House of the Soul* (Methuen).
189	9	*Ibid.*
189	18	Aldous Huxley, *Grey Eminence* (Chatto & Windus).
190	7	*The Cloud of Unknowing*, a version in modern English of the fourteenth-century classic (New York: Harper).
190	10	*The Guide to True Peace* (New York: Harper).

CHAPTER 15. *The Life of Communion*

191	3	Dylan Thomas, *Collected Poems* (J. M. Dent). Used by permission.
192	7	H. L. Jackson, "Faith," *Hasting's Dictionary of Christ and the Gospels*, I.
193	2	William Ralph Inge, *Christian Mysticism* (Longmans).
193	7	Richard Roberts, *The Discipline of Interior Prayer* (New York: Association Press).
193	18	"Oned" is the term used by the fourteenth-century English contemplatives.
193	23	Inge, *op. cit.*
193	25	F. Augustine Baker, *Holy Wisdom* (New York: Harper).
193	31	Inge, *op. cit.*
194	3	*Ibid.*
194	7	*Ibid.*
194	17	Buber, *op. cit.*
194	24	Cited in Inge, *op. cit.*
195	4	*Meister Eckhart*, tr. and ed. Raymond Bernard Blakney (New York: Harper).
194	11	Inge, *op. cit.*
194	13	*Ibid.*
195	16	The three most noted scholars to insist upon the distinction are Rufus Jones, Baron F. von Hügel, and Dean W. R. Inge. Albert Schweitzer has an extended discussion of world-denying and world-affirming mysticism, to which I am greatly indebted, in his *Indian Thought and Its Development* (A. & C. Black).

PAGE	LINE	
195	27	*Theologia Germanica*.
196	17	W. B. Yeats, "Introduction" to Rabindranath Tagore, *Gitanjali* (Boston: International Pocket Library).
196	30	Baker, *op. cit.*
197	11	W. R. Inge, *Light, Life, and Love*, Selections from the German mystics of the middle ages (Methuen).
197	14	*Ibid.*
197	20	Martin Buber, *Between Man and Man* (Routledge).
197	31	*Ibid.*
198	18	Huxley, *Perennial Philosophy*.
198	22	Huxley, *Ape and Essence* (Chatto & Windus). Used by permission.
198	30	Gen. 1:31.
198	31	Ps. 24:1.
199	5	Inge, *Christian Mysticism*.
200	7	*The Cloud of Unknowing*, E. Underhill, ed. (Watkins).
200	12	*Ibid.*
200	15	*Ibid.*
200	20	*Ibid.*
200	23	*Ibid.*
200	27	Richard Baxter, *The Saint's Everlasting Rest* (New York: Robert Carter).
201	1	*Guide to True Peace.*
201	19	Eliot, *Four Quartets* (Faber & Faber). Used by permission.
202	26	Augustine, *Confessions*, bk. ix.
203	19	John Milton, "At a Solemn Music," line 6.
203	20	St. John of the Cross, *op. cit.*, I.
203	26	*The Cloud of Unknowing.*
204	3	*Ibid.* The spelling is modernized in this citation.
204	5	Cited by Underhill, *Mysticism*.
204	19	Baron F. von Hügel, *The Mystical Element of Religion as Studied in Saint Catherine of Genoa and Her Friends* (J. M. Dent).
204	24	*Ibid.*
204	33	*Ibid.*
205	21	Isa. 11:6, 9 (Smith-Goodspeed).
206	4	*The Cloud of Unknowing.*
206	24	St. John of the Cross, *op. cit.*, II.
207	14	Cited by Inge, *Christian Mysticism*.
207	32	Henry Suso, "Suso and His Spiritual Daughter," in Inge, *Light, Life, and Love*.
209	7	In private conversation with the author.
209	13	Underhill, *House of the Soul*.

PAGE	LINE	
210	4	Luke 12:50 (Moffatt).
210	9	Buber, *Tales of the Hasidim*, I.
210	29	Brother Lawrence, *The Practice of the Presence of God*, Douglas Steere, ed. (Nashville: Upper Room).
211	12	*Ibid.*
211	27	*Ibid.*
211	30	*Ibid.*
212	4	*Ibid.*
212	33	Frank Laubach, *Letters by a Modern Mystic* (Lutterworth).
213	2	*Ibid.*
213	16	*Ibid.*
214	18	St. Bonaventura, *Life of St. Francis* (New York: Dutton).
214	28	Eliot, *Four Quartets* (Faber & Faber). Used by permission.

Index